It Happened This Month

Herb Klischies

TEACH Services, Inc.
PUBLISHING
www.TEACHServices.com • (800) 367-1844

World rights reserved. This book or any portion thereof may not be copied or reproduced in any form or manner whatever, except as provided by law, without the written permission of the publisher, except by a reviewer who may quote brief passages in a review.

The author assumes full responsibility for the accuracy of all facts and quotations as cited in this book. The opinions expressed in this book are the author's personal views and interpretations, and do not necessarily reflect those of the publisher.

Copyright © 2017 Herb Klischies

Copyright © 2017 TEACH Services, Inc.

ISBN-13: 978-1-4796-0729-7 (Paperback)

ISBN-13: 978-1-4796-0730-3 (ePub)

ISBN-13: 978-1-4796-0731-0 (Mobi)

Library of Congress Control Number: 2017900770

Table of Contents

All facts, dates, and events used in this book were accurate at the time of original publication (1957-1980).

1957 5	1969 97
1958 9	1970 105
1959 17	1971 113
1960 25	1972 121
1961 33	1973 129
1962 41	1974 137
1963 49	1975 145
1964 57	1976 153
1965 65	1977 161
1966 73	1978 169
1967 81	1979 177
1968 89	1980 187

1957

Nineteen Fifty-Seven

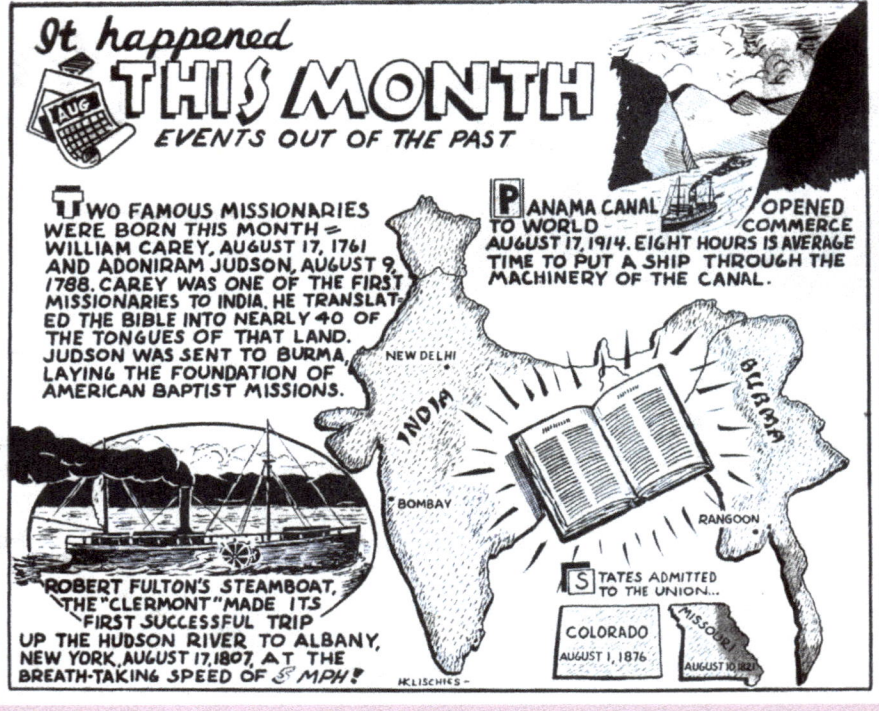

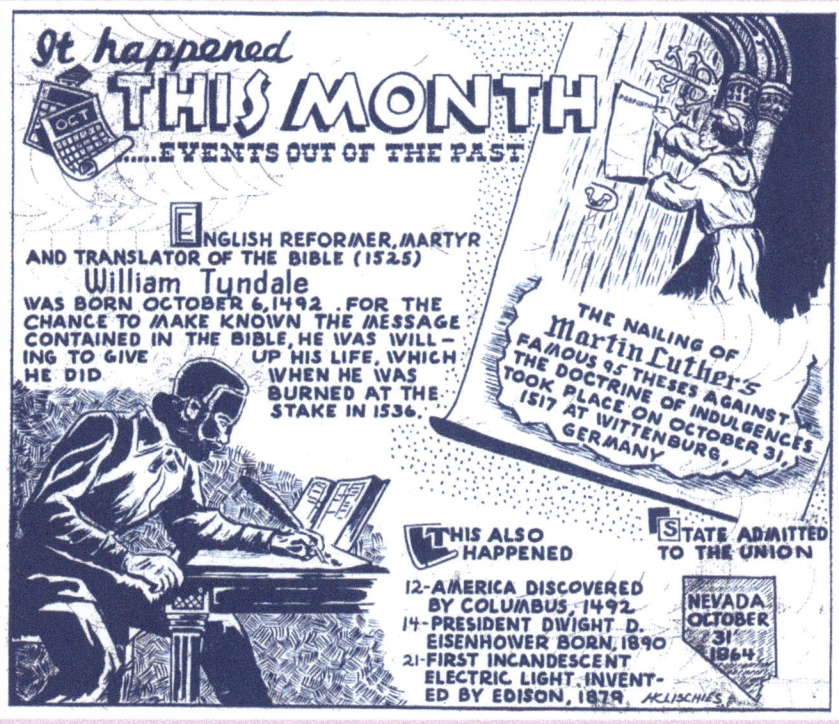

1958

Nineteen Fifty-Eight

1958 • Page 11

Page 12 • 1958

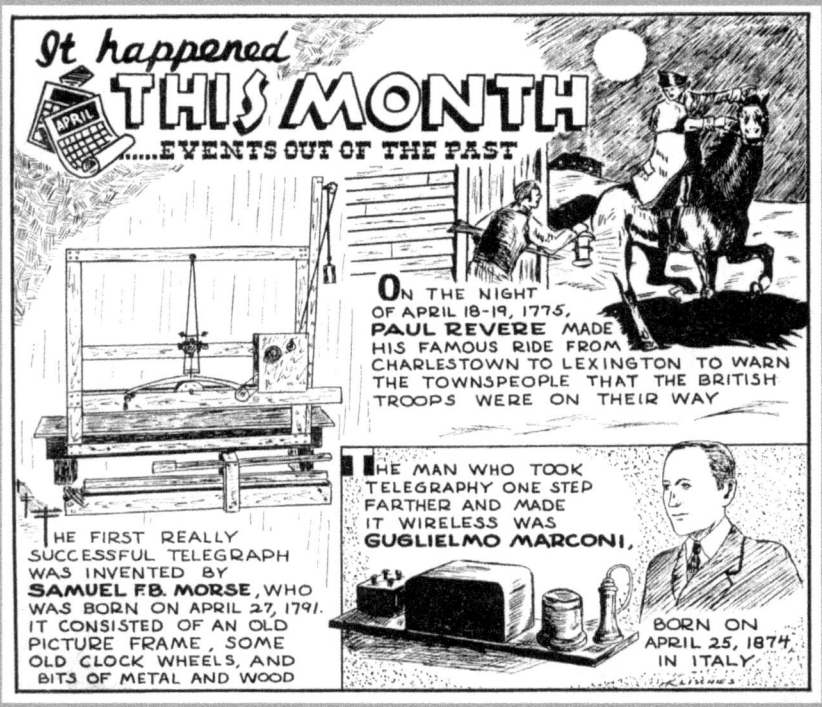

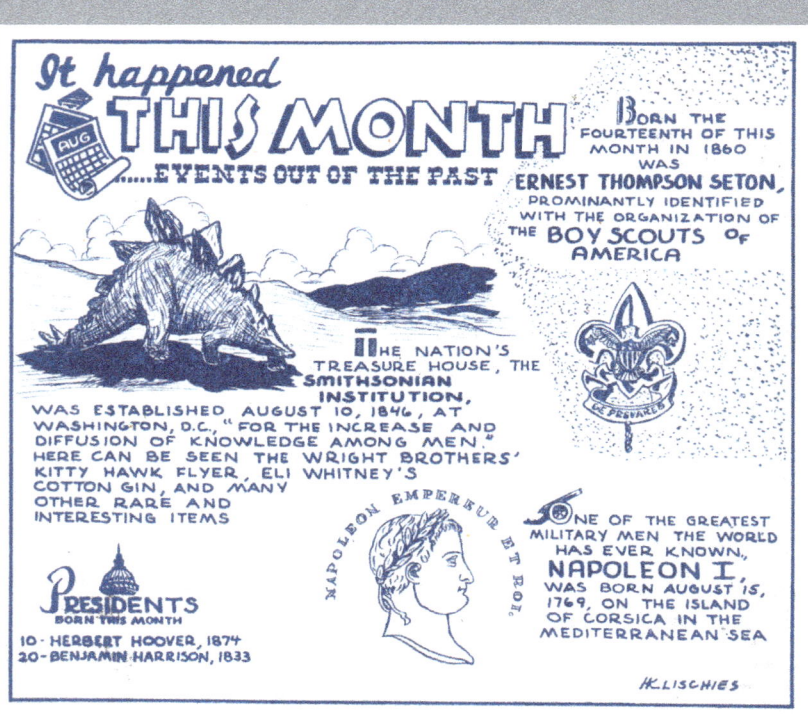

1959

Nineteen Fifty-Nine

1959 • Page 19

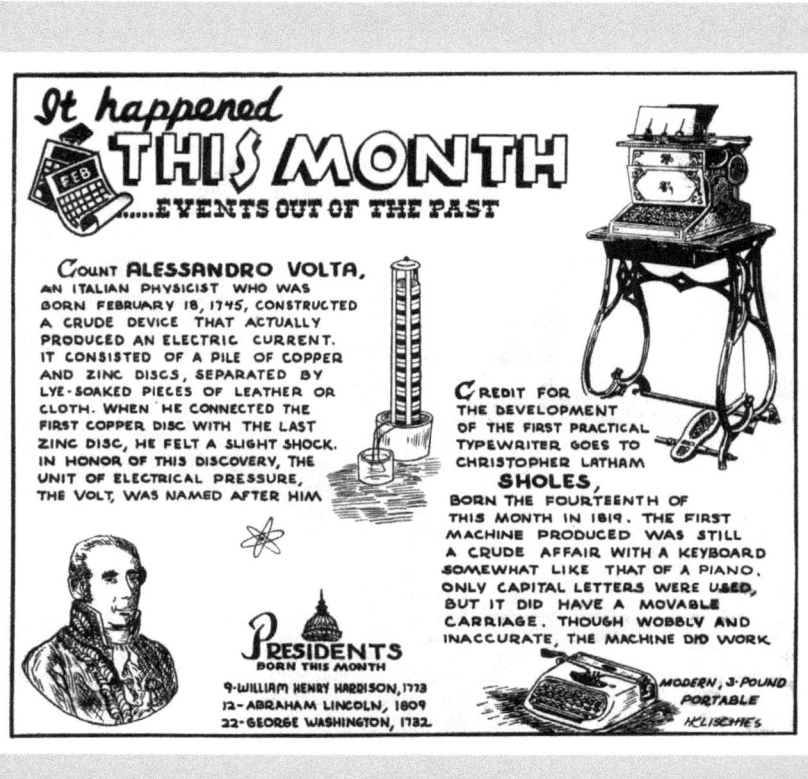

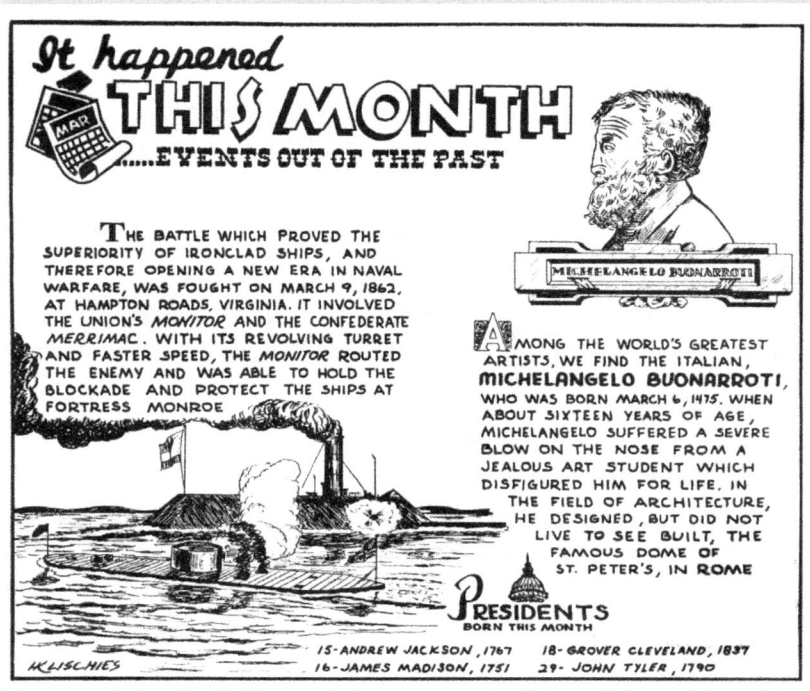

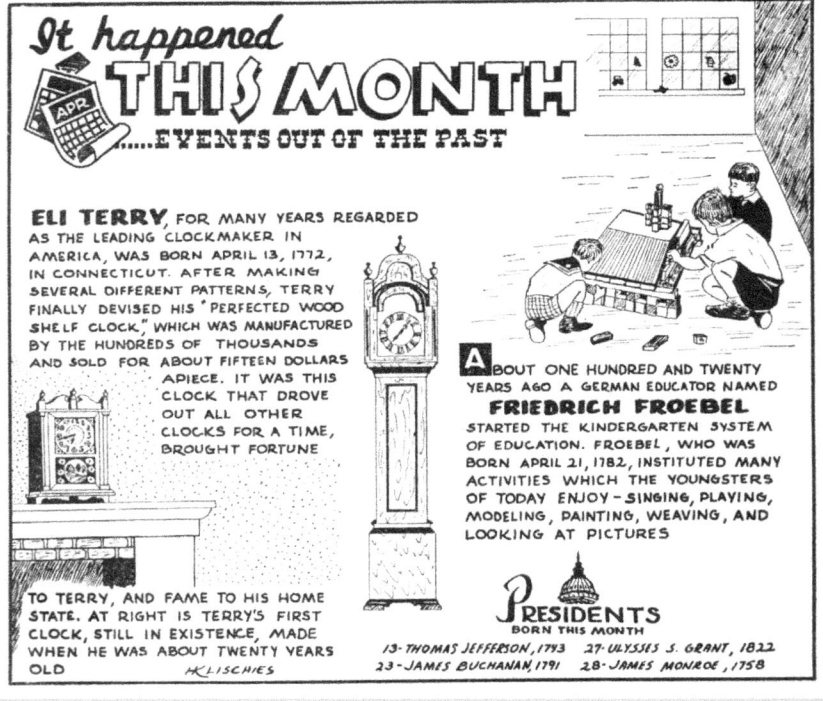

1960

Nineteen Sixty

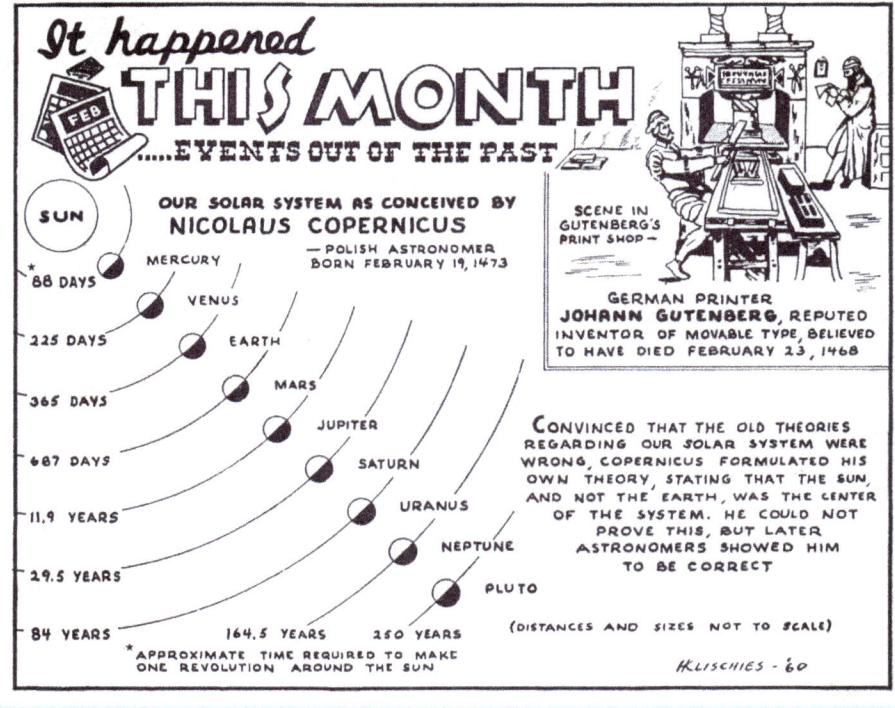

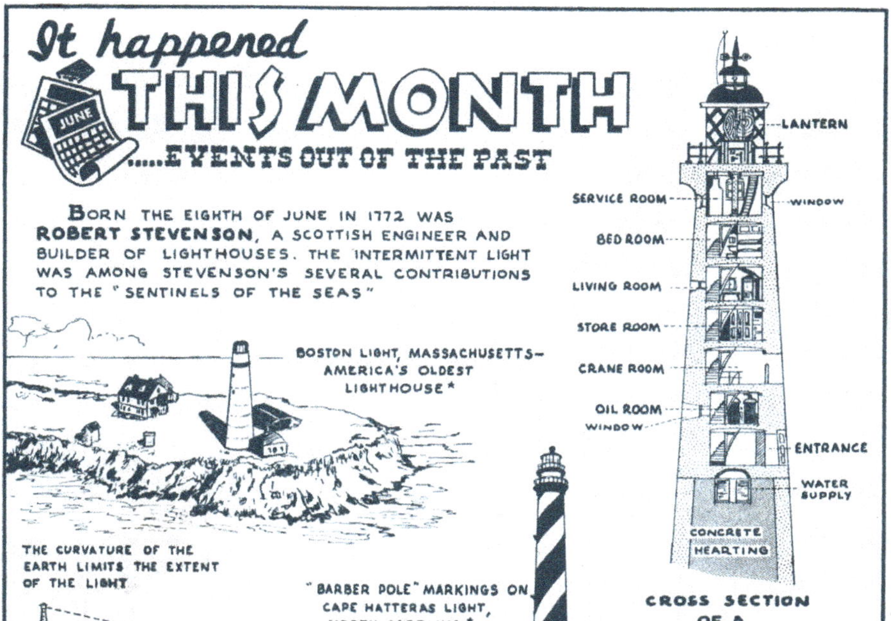

1961

Nineteen Sixty-One

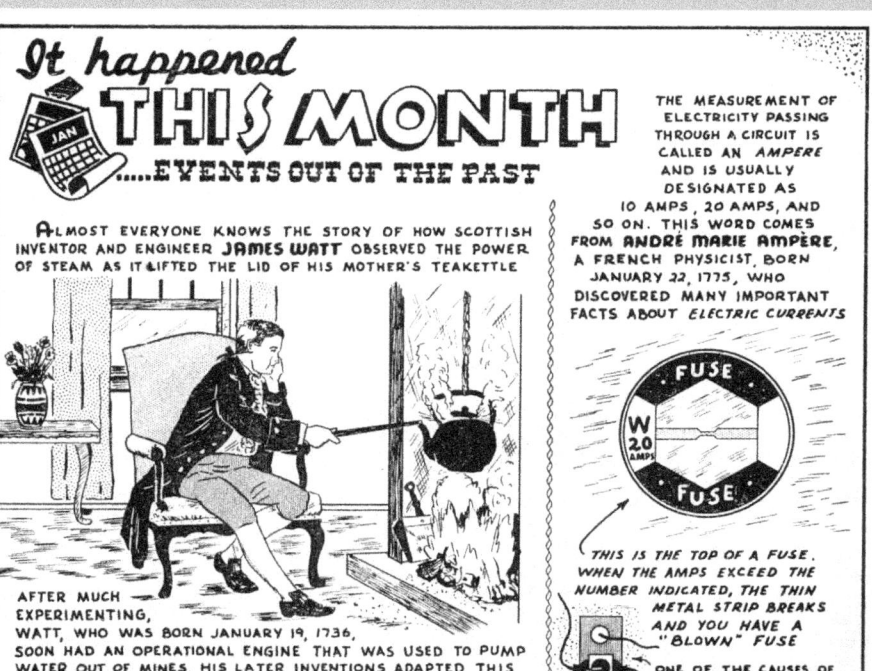

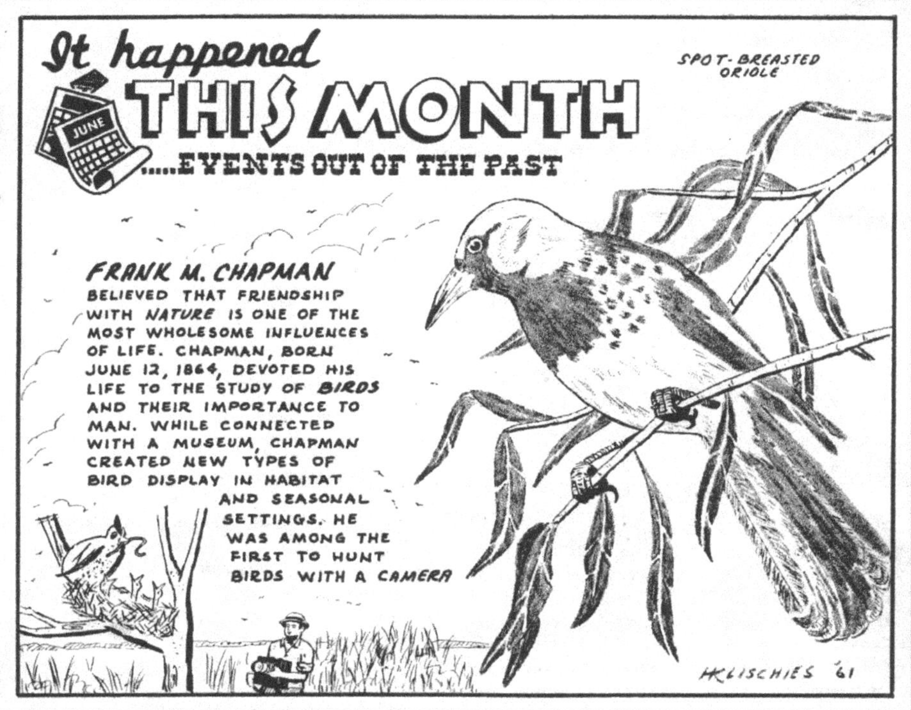

Page 38 • 1961

1962

Nineteen Sixty-Two

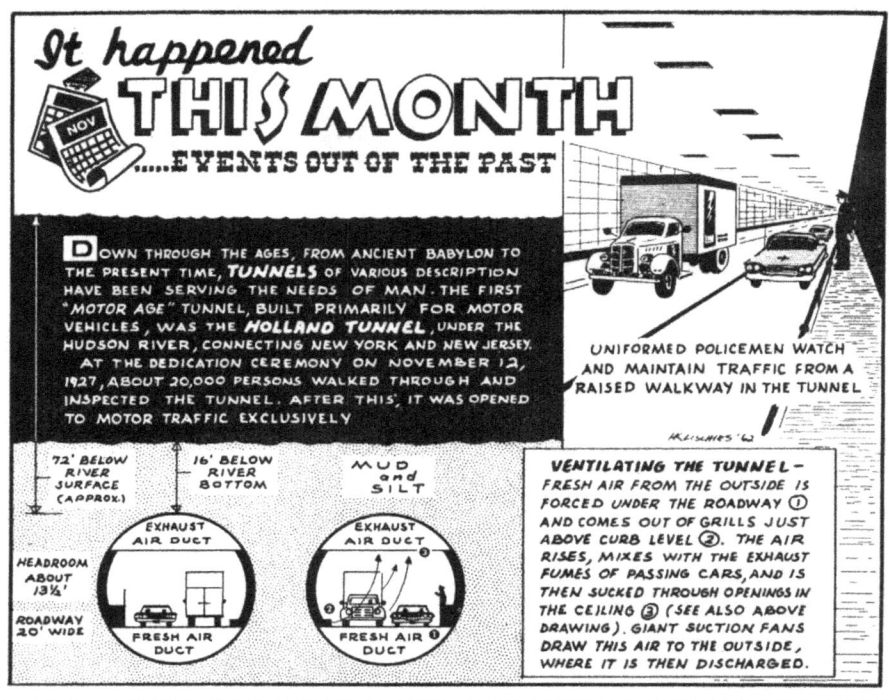

1963

Nineteen Sixty-Three

1963 • Page 51

It Happened THIS MONTH
...EVENTS OUT OF THE PAST

JAN

FIRST PUBLIC DEMONSTRATION OF X-RAYS

FULL SIZE X-RAY ON ONE PIECE OF FILM

WILHELM KONRAD ROENTGEN
1845-1923

TODAY, WHENEVER SOMETHING INSIDE US HURTS, WE GO TO THE DOCTOR OR DENTIST WHO, WITH THE HELP OF AN X-RAY PICTURE, DETERMINES WHETHER WE NEED AN OPERATION OR WHETHER AN ACHING TOOTH NEEDS TO COME OUT. THE DISCOVERY OF X-RAYS WAS MADE PUBLIC JANUARY 23, 1896, BY THE GERMAN SCIENTIST **WILHELM KONRAD ROENTGEN.** WITH THESE RAYS, SURGEONS ARE ABLE TO LOOK THROUGH THE FLESH AND SEE WHAT IS GOING ON INSIDE THEIR PATIENTS.

X-RAYS ARE ALSO USED IN INDUSTRY TO SPOT DEFECTS

X-RAYING A HUGE DIESEL ENGINE CRANKSHAFT

KLISCHIES '63

It Happened THIS MONTH
...EVENTS OUT OF THE PAST

FEB

GASPARD DE COLIGNY II
Leader of the French Huguenots

ADMIRAL GASPARD DE COLIGNY II, A FRENCHMAN, WAS CAPTURED BY THE SPANISH IN THE INVASION OF SAINT-QUENTIN AND IMPRISONED. WHILE IN PRISON HE WAS CONVERTED TO THE TEACHINGS OF *JOHN CALVIN*. AFTER HIS RELEASE, COLIGNY BECAME A LEADER OF THE **HUGUENOTS**. A NUMBER OF RELIGIOUS BATTLES TOOK PLACE BETWEEN THE HUGUENOTS AND THE CATHOLICS, BUT COLIGNY MANAGED TO KEEP HIS ARMY TOGETHER IN SPITE OF SEVERAL DEFEATS.

IN THE RELIGIOUS STRUGGLES OF EUROPE DURING THE SIXTEENTH AND SEVENTEENTH CENTURIES, ONE GROUP OF PROTESTANTS STANDS OUT AS PROMINENTLY AS ANY— **THE HUGUENOTS OF FRANCE**

COLIGNY, BORN FEBRUARY 15, 1519, WAS WOUNDED BY AN ASSASSIN'S BULLET IN AUGUST, 1572. THE KING, FEARING A GENERAL HUGUENOT UPRISING TO AVENGE THE ATTEMPTED ASSASSINATION, AGREED TO KILL THE HUGUENOT LEADERS. THIS WAS THE INFAMOUS MASSACRE OF *SAINT BARTHOLOMEW'S DAY*, AUGUST 24, 1572, WHICH WAS THE SIGNAL FOR OPEN PERSECUTION OF ALL PROTESTANTS THROUGHOUT ALL OF FRANCE. IT WASN'T UNTIL MUCH LATER (ABOUT 1700) THAT THIS PERSECUTION FINALLY ENDED.

Page 52 • 1963

1963 • Page 53

It Happened THIS MONTH
...EVENTS OUT OF THE PAST

DEFEAT OF THE SPANISH ARMADA

During the months of July and August, 1588, a sea battle was fought between England and Spain, the outcome of which was to reach down to our present day. **THE SPANISH ARMADA** was the great fleet sent to invade and conquer England. But the English met the Spaniards with determination and force, and defeated them.

FROM A DUTCH PAINTING

Had Spain succeeded in her plan to invade England, and gone on to colonize North America, it is almost certain that the United States would have developed as a Catholic nation. But with Spain defeated, England colonized North America and gave to the United States a Protestant heritage.

KLISCHIES '63

It Happened THIS MONTH
...EVENTS OUT OF THE PAST

KRAKATOA — Violence in Nature

One of the most violent volcanic eruptions in recorded human history took place in 1883 on the uninhabited island of **KRAKATOA**, between Sumatra and Java.

Following the eruption, great waves swept the coastal cities of Java and Sumatra with such force that many were destroyed. It has been estimated that 36,000 people lost their lives during this time of destruction.

The dust cloud from the eruption produced the most beautiful sunsets all over the world for many months.

Supposedly extinct for 200 years, the volcano started rumbling one day and continued for several months. Suddenly, on August 26, a tremendous explosion took place, followed by a series of explosions ending on August 28. The catastrophe blew up two thirds of the main island.

It wasn't until two years after the explosion that all the volcanic particles finally settled back down to earth.

KLISCHIES '63

1963 • Page 55

It Happened THIS MONTH
...EVENTS OUT OF THE PAST

SEWING MACHINE by Elias Howe, Jr.

ONE ITEM INCLUDED ON EVERY LIST OF GREAT INVENTIONS IS THE *SEWING MACHINE*. MANY MACHINISTS, INVENTORS, AND HOBBYISTS TRIED THEIR HAND AT BUILDING THE *PERFECT* SEWING MACHINE. THE MODEL AT RIGHT WAS BUILT BY *ELIAS HOWE, JR*, AND PATENTED SEPTEMBER 10, 1846. THESE EARLY MODELS UNDERWENT MANY CHANGES THROUGH THE YEARS UNTIL TODAY WE HAVE MACHINES THAT CAN GO BACKWARD, FORWARD, MAKE BUTTONHOLES, DO FANCY STITCHES, AND ARE LIGHTWEIGHT AND PORTABLE.

KLISCHIES '63

SEVERAL EARLY-MODEL SEWING MACHINES AND THEIR INVENTORS —

J.A. DODGE - 1818   J. BACHELDER - 1849   LEROW & BLODGETT - 1877   I.M. SINGER - 1851

It Happened THIS MONTH
...EVENTS OUT OF THE PAST

World War I Flying Ace — CAPT. EDDIE RICKENBACKER

FAMOUS HAT-IN-THE-RING SYMBOL USED ON RICKENBACKER'S AIRPLANE

OCTOBER 8, 1890, MARKS THE BIRTHDAY OF AMERICA'S WORLD WAR I ACE —

CAPT. EDDIE RICKENBACKER.

WITH HIS *SPAD XIII* (SIMILAR TO THE ONE SHOWN AT LEFT), RICKENBACKER SHOT DOWN 26 OF THE ENEMY'S PLANES TO BECOME AMERICA'S

AIR ACE.

IN WORLD WAR II, A PLANE CARRYING RICKENBACKER WAS FORCED DOWN INTO THE PACIFIC OCEAN. THE MEN DRIFTED IN OPEN LIFE RAFTS FOR 22 DAYS BEFORE BEING RESCUED. THEY HELD A PRAYER MEETING EVERY DAY, READING MATTHEW 6:31-34 TO STRENGTHEN THEM.

KLISCHIES '63

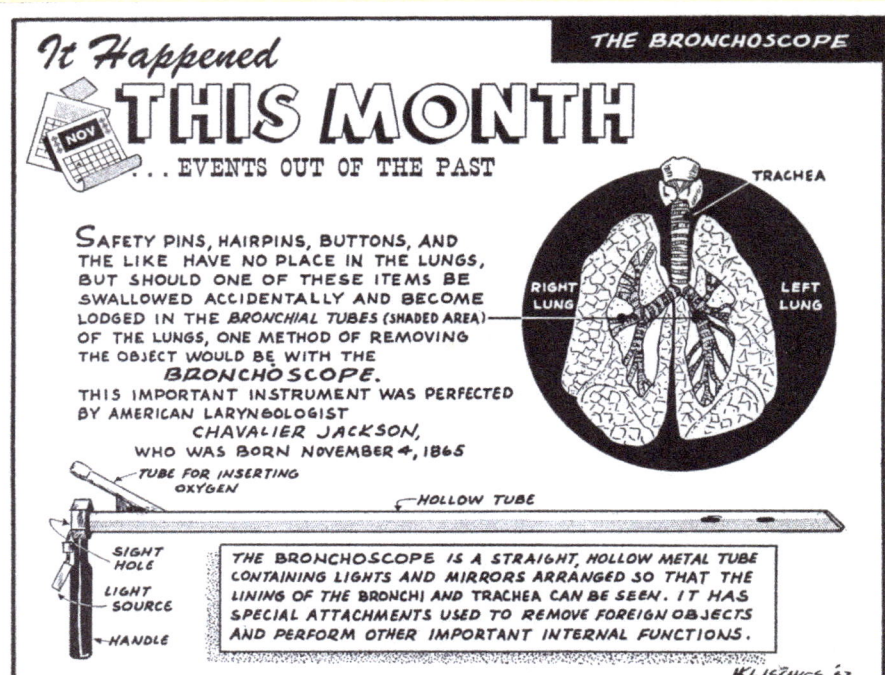

1964

Nineteen Sixty-Four

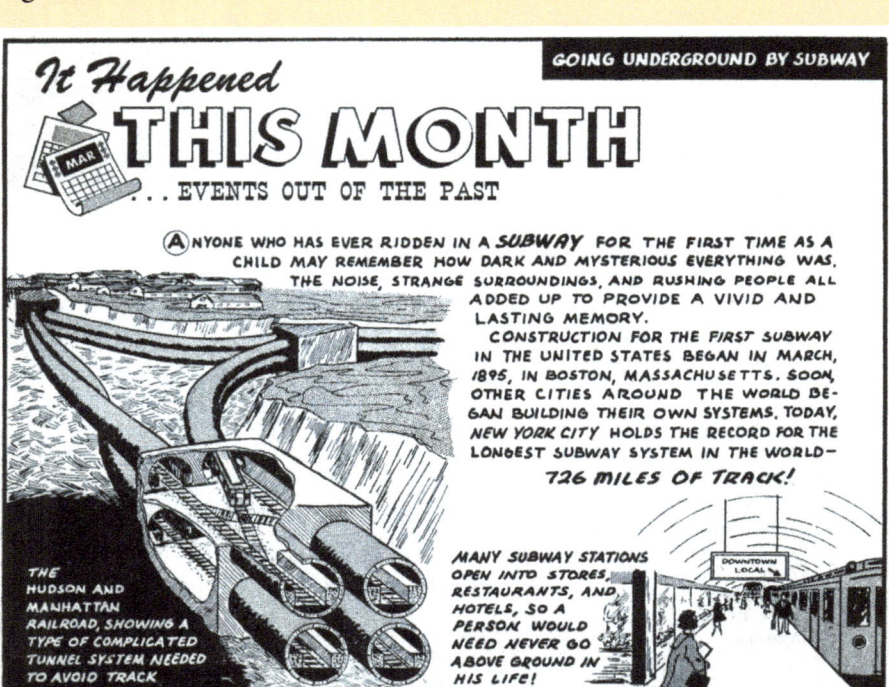

It Happened THIS MONTH
...EVENTS OUT OF THE PAST

MAY

FIRST MAN TO THE NORTH POLE

BEING THE FIRST TO DISCOVER THE *NORTH POLE* WAS AN IDEA THAT HAD FASCINATED MEN FOR ALMOST 400 YEARS. THIS FEAT WAS FINALLY ACCOMPLISHED IN APRIL, 1909, BY VETERAN AMERICAN ARCTIC EXPLORER **ROBERT E. PEARY** (BORN MAY 6, 1856)

TO MAKE CERTAIN HE WAS TRULY AT THE "TOP OF THE WORLD," PEARY TRAVELED SEVERAL MILES IN VARIOUS DIRECTIONS, CROSSING AND CRISSCROSSING THE "TOP"

SINCE HE AND HIS MEN WOULD BE LIVING IN THE LAND OF THE *ESKIMO*, PEARY REASONED, WHY NOT LIVE AND DRESS AS THEY DID? SNOW HOUSES WERE BUILT, WHICH PROVED WARMER AND STRONGER AGAINST THE WIND THAN TENTS. FOR CLOTHING, ALL DRESSED IN LIGHT, FLEXIBLE, AND VERY WARM ESKIMO SUITS MADE OF ANIMAL FUR.

FOR *FOOD*, PEARY BORROWED AN IDEA FROM THE AMERICAN INDIANS. "*PEMMICAN*," A HIGHLY CONCENTRATED PREPARATION, CONSISTED OF *DRIED BUFFALO MEAT*, POUNDED FINE AND MIXED WITH *MELTED FAT*. A SIMILAR PREPARATION USED FOR EMERGENCY RATIONS BY THE EXPLORERS CONTAINED *DRIED BEEF, FLOUR, MOLASSES*, AND *SUET*.

It Happened THIS MONTH
...EVENTS OUT OF THE PAST

JUNE

SEISMOGRAPH EXHIBITED

"...AND THERE SHALL BE...EARTHQUAKES, IN DIVERS PLACES." MATT. 24:7

THE RECENT DESTRUCTIVE *EARTHQUAKE* IN ALASKA AGAIN REMINDS US THAT WE ARE LIVING IN THE TIME OF THE END OF THIS EARTH'S HISTORY. EARTHQUAKES ARE, FOR THE MOST PART, IMPOSSIBLE TO PREDICT, BUT SCIENTISTS DO KNOW THE *REGIONS* WHERE THEY ARE LIKELY TO OCCUR. (THE SAN ANDREAS FAULT, IN CALIFORNIA, IS A PROBABLE AREA FOR FUTURE QUAKES.)

SAN FRANCISCO
LOS ANGELES
SAN DIEGO

SUDDEN MOVEMENTS OF ROCK BENEATH THE EARTH ARE THE MAIN CAUSES OF EARTHQUAKES. ROCKS AND EARTH MAY SLIP IN ANY DIRECTION, CAUSING TIDAL WAVES AND LANDSLIDES.

EARTH'S CRUST
SIDEWAYS
DOWNWARD

A SIMPLE SEISMOGRAPH

AN INSTRUMENT CALLED A *SEISMOGRAPH* RECORDS THE INTENSITY AND FOCUS OF A QUAKE. SUCH A SEISMOGRAPH WAS EXHIBITED AT THE *LICK OBSERVATORY*, IN CALIFORNIA, JUNE 1, 1888.

HEAVY WEIGHT
ROTATING CYLINDER
WRITING PEN
INTENSITY OF EARTHQUAKE RECORDED ON CYLINDER
DIRECTION OF QUAKES

1965

Nineteen Sixty-Five

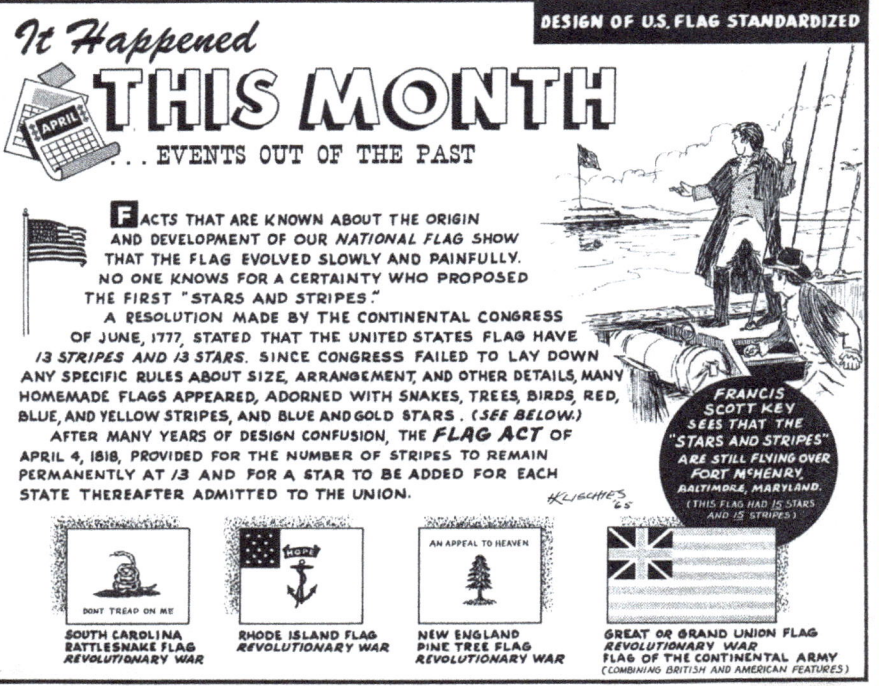

It Happened THIS MONTH
...EVENTS OUT OF THE PAST

DEVELOPMENT OF LOCKS AND KEYS

MAN HAS NEEDED **LOCKS** FROM EARLIEST TIMES TO PROTECT HIS WEALTH AND PROPERTY FROM THIEVES. A 4,000-YEAR-OLD WOODEN LOCK WAS FOUND NEAR THE SITE OF ANCIENT NINEVEH. THE *EGYPTIANS* USED BRASS AND LATER IRON. ROMAN LOCKS WERE MOSTLY MADE OF IRON, BUT RUST HAS PREVENTED ANY LOCK FROM SURVIVING IN ITS ENTIRETY.

AN EGYPTIAN LOCK AND KEY

SOME LOCKS REQUIRED VERY LONG KEYS - AS MUCH AS 3 FEET LONG! THESE WERE CARRIED ON THE CUSTODIAN'S SHOULDER, AND COULD BE USED AS A WEAPON.

PORTABLE LOCKS, OR **PADLOCKS**, WERE MADE IN THE SHAPE OF ANIMALS, FISH, OR FOWL.

COMBINATION PADLOCK

IT REMAINED FOR AMERICAN PORTRAIT PAINTER **LINUS YALE, JR.**, TO DEVELOP THE FAMOUS **PIN-TUMBLER CYLINDER LOCK**. YALE RECEIVED A PATENT MAY 6, 1851, ON A LOCK AND KEY HE HAD PERFECTED.

OPERATION OF PIN-TUMBLER LOCK:
1. PINS EXTEND INTO A GROOVE IN THE LOCK CYLINDER, BEING HELD DOWN BY SPRINGS.
2. WHEN THE PROPER KEY IS INSERTED, TUMBLERS RISE TO PROPER HEIGHT, ALLOWING CYLINDER (A) TO BE ROTATED, OPENING THE DOOR.

THIS LOCK WAS AN IMMEDIATE SUCCESS, BECAUSE IT COULD BE MASS-PRODUCED, NEEDED ONLY A SHORT KEY, AND HAD A HIGH DEGREE OF SECURITY.

BESIDES GUARDING PROPERTY, LOCKS ALSO PERFORMED SOME GRUESOME OPERATIONS. FINGERS OF WOULD-BE THIEVES WERE CUT OFF OR PRICKED WITH POISONED NEEDLES. ONE CHEST SHOT A PISTOL STRAIGHT AT ANYONE TAMPERING WITH THE LOCK.

KLISCHIES '65

It Happened THIS MONTH
...EVENTS OUT OF THE PAST

LOOKOUT TOWERS TO SPOT FIRES

OUR *NATIONAL FORESTS* PROVIDE MANY IMPORTANT RESOURCES - WOOD, WATER, WILDLIFE, AND *RECREATION*. BUT ALL THIS CAN BE DESTROYED IN A MATTER OF HOURS BY *FIRE* - STARTED EITHER CARELESSLY BY CAMPERS OR BY LIGHTNING.

ONE METHOD OF EARLY FIRE DETECTION IS BY THE **LOOKOUT TOWER**. THESE TOWERS ARE MANNED BY PEOPLE TRAINED TO SPOT AND REPORT FIRES AS SOON AS THEY START.

THE FIRST LOOKOUT TOWER WAS PUT INTO SERVICE IN JUNE, 1905, ON SQUAW MOUNTAIN IN MAINE. IT CONSISTED OF A LOG CABIN WITH A FLAT ROOF. TODAY, IN ADDITION TO THE TOWER, OTHER METHODS OF FIRE DETECTION INCLUDE THE USE OF AIRPLANES AND HELICOPTERS.

CAMPING TIME IS HERE! MAKE SURE *YOUR* FIRE IS OUT WHEN YOU LEAVE YOUR CAMPSITE. DOUSE WITH WATER AND COVER WITH DIRT.

KLISCHIES '65

ONE TYPE OF LOOKOUT TOWER, SET HIGH ON A HILL. THE FIRE WATCHERS CAN SEE MANY MILES IN ANY DIRECTION.

1965 • Page 71

1966

Nineteen Sixty-Six

It Happened THIS MONTH
...EVENTS OUT OF THE PAST

MOUNT PALOMAR MIRROR — A GIANT STEP FORWARD IN THE FIELD OF ASTRONOMY

How would you like to mix up about 20 TONS of batter and bake ONE WAFFLE in a waffle iron 17 FEET in diameter? This is about the best way to describe the manufacture of the 200-INCH MIRROR used in the giant reflecting telescope of MOUNT PALOMAR, in California. On March 25, 1934, the CORNING GLASS WORKS, of Corning, New York, began the complex operation by pouring the molten glass into the mold. Trouble developed and this first disk became useless as a mirror. It is now on exhibition at the Corning Glass Museum.

In a REFLECTING TELESCOPE, light is reflected by the large mirror ① to a smaller mirror ② to the eyepiece ③.

A SECOND DISK WAS POURED AND AFTER 10 MONTHS OF COOLING WAS READY TO BE SHIPPED TO CALIFORNIA.

NUMEROUS SHIPPING PROBLEMS DELAYED THE DEPARTURE OF THE GLASS. ON MARCH 26, 1936, IT FINALLY LEFT CORNING ON A SPECIAL FLATCAR AND WAS DELIVERED TO THE MOUNT PALOMAR OPTICAL SHOPS FOR THE GRINDING AND POLISHING.

MOUNT PALOMAR — HOME OF THE 200-INCH TELESCOPE

It Happened THIS MONTH
...EVENTS OUT OF THE PAST

CLARA BARTON — FOUNDER OF THE AMERICAN NATIONAL RED CROSS

"ANGEL OF THE BATTLEFIELD"

One of the most famous nurses ever, CLARA BARTON earned the title "ANGEL OF THE BATTLEFIELD" for her heroic and selfless dedication to the task of caring for the sick and wounded soldiers all during the CIVIL WAR. She saw herself more as a provider than a nurse — her kettles of hot gruel and mush were very welcome sights after a hard battle.

ON TWO OCCASIONS SHE NEARLY LOST HER LIFE WHEN SHELL FRAGMENTS RIPPED THROUGH HER CLOTHING WHILE SHE WAS TENDING THE WOUNDED.

AS A RESULT OF HER SUGGESTIONS, THE AMERICAN RED CROSS, WHICH SHE FOUNDED, WAS PERMITTED NOT ONLY TO GIVE AID IN TIME OF WAR BUT ALSO TO PROVIDE AID AND COMFORT IN THE WAKE OF PEACETIME CALAMITIES, SUCH AS FLOODS AND EARTHQUAKES.

MISS BARTON'S HOME IN GLEN ECHO, MARYLAND, WHERE SHE DIED, APRIL 12, 1912, IS OPEN TO THE PUBLIC.

It Happened THIS MONTH
...Events Out of the Past

AMERICAN BIBLE SOCIETY

150TH ANNIVERSARY 1816–1966

THIS YEAR MARKS THE 150th ANNIVERSARY OF THE *AMERICAN BIBLE SOCIETY*. FOUNDED MAY 11, 1816, IN NEW YORK CITY, THE AMERICAN BIBLE SOCIETY HAS, THROUGH THE YEARS, CARRIED ON A PROGRAM OF TRANSLATION, PRODUCTION, DISTRIBUTION, AND ENCOURAGING THE USE OF THE *HOLY SCRIPTURES* IN THE UNITED STATES AND 130 OTHER COUNTRIES.

THE BIBLE IS ALSO PRODUCED IN BRAILLE FOR THE BLIND. HERE IS THE COMPLETE BIBLE IN 20 VOLUMES AND WEIGHING 90 POUNDS!

~The Year of the Bible~
1966 HAS BEEN DESIGNATED AS "THE YEAR OF THE BIBLE" AS PART OF THE 150TH ANNIVERSARY OF THE AMERICAN BIBLE SOCIETY. THE AMERICAN PEOPLE ARE BEING URGED TO READ THEIR BIBLES DAILY. *JUNIORS SHOULD BE DOING THIS ALREADY!*

ALL OVER THIS TROUBLED WORLD, THE *AMERICAN BIBLE SOCIETY* HAS DEDICATED WORKERS CARRYING THE WORD OF GOD TO THE PEOPLE. HERE IS A "BIBLE VAN" IN SOUTH INDIA.

KLISCHIES '66

It Happened THIS MONTH
...Events Out of the Past

BALLOON CORPS ESTABLISHED

AMERICA'S FIRST AIR FORCE CONSISTED NOT OF AN ARMADA OF AIRPLANES, BUT OF *SEVEN* OBSERVATION BALLOONS. THE *BALLOON CORPS OF THE ARMY OF THE POTOMAC* HAD ITS BEGINNING JUNE 18, 1861, WHEN AMERICAN PROFESSOR *THADDEUS LOWE* CONVINCED PRESIDENT LINCOLN OF THE VALUE OF LIGHTER-THAN-AIR CRAFT BY SENDING HIM A TELEGRAM FROM A BALLOON 500 FEET OVER THE CITY OF WASHINGTON, D.C.

DISADVANTAGES OF THE BALLOON INCLUDED THE TIME AND BULKY EQUIPMENT NEEDED TO PUT IT INTO SERVICE. ON SEVERAL OCCASIONS THE BALLOON COULDN'T BE USED BECAUSE IT WASN'T AVAILABLE WHEN NEEDED.

PATCHES OF SILK DRESSES USED IN THE MAKING OF BALLOONS. IT TOOK MANY SUCH PATCHES TO MAKE ONE BALLOON.

BECAUSE OF LACK OF INTEREST BY THE MILITARY GENERALS, THE BALLOON CORPS WAS DISBANDED IN JUNE, 1863.

UP GOES THE *INTREPID*, WHOSE OBSERVER WILL SPOT FOR THE UNION FORCES

KLISCHIES '66

It Happened THIS MONTH
...EVENTS OUT OF THE PAST

COUNT FERDINAND von ZEPPELIN
BUILDER OF AIRSHIPS — BORN JULY 8, 1838

LAST MONTH WE NOTED THE DEVELOPMENT OF LIGHTER-THAN-AIR CRAFT BY FEATURING BALLOONS. IT WASN'T LONG BEFORE AIRSHIPS TOOK TO THE SKIES. PERHAPS THE MOST FAMOUS AIRSHIP BUILDER OF ALL WAS GERMAN COUNT VON ZEPPELIN. IN FACT - AIRSHIPS ARE CALLED ZEPPELINS IN HONOR OF THIS EARLY PIONEER.

A RIDE IN A ZEPPELIN WAS ONE OF LEISURE AND LUXURY. WITH TRAVEL BEING MUCH SLOWER THAN BY AIRPLANE (ABOUT 60-70 MILES PER HOUR), THE PASSING SCENERY BELOW COULD BE THOROUGHLY ENJOYED FROM THE WIDE PANORAMIC WINDOWS.
THIS SHOWS A TYPICAL PASSENGER CABIN ON THE GRAF ZEPPELIN.

INTEREST IN ZEPPELINS WAS GREATEST DURING THE LATE 1920's AND EARLY 1930's, BUT SEVERAL UNFORTUNATE DISASTERS AND INCREASING SPEEDS OF AIRPLANES PUT A QUICK END TO THIS ONCE DELIGHTFUL MEANS OF TRAVEL.

THE TRAGIC HINDENBURG DISASTER AT LAKEHURST, NEW JERSEY, MAY, 1937, WITH A LOSS OF 36 LIVES.

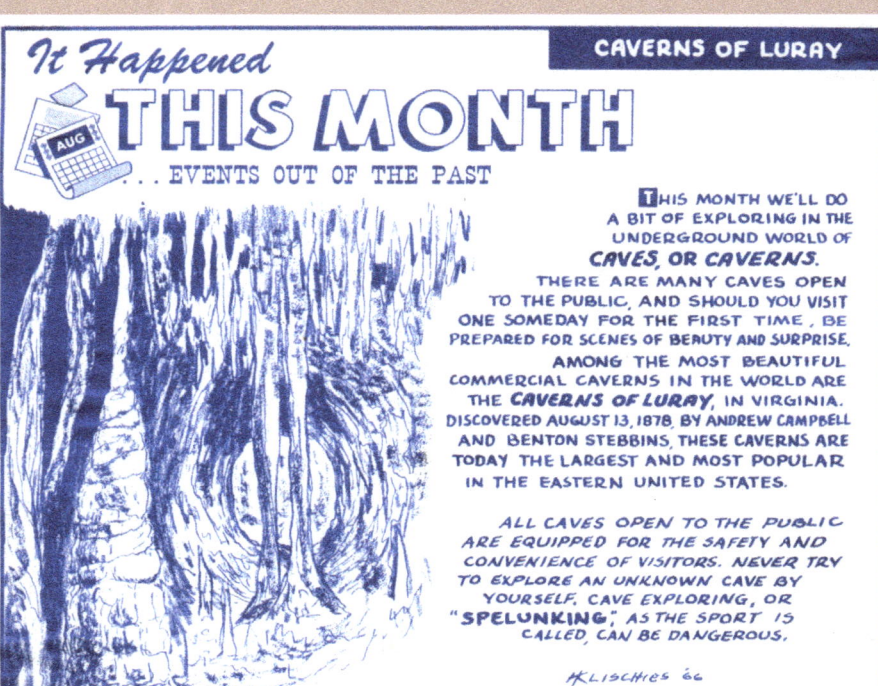

It Happened THIS MONTH
...EVENTS OUT OF THE PAST

CAVERNS OF LURAY

THIS MONTH WE'LL DO A BIT OF EXPLORING IN THE UNDERGROUND WORLD OF CAVES, OR CAVERNS.
THERE ARE MANY CAVES OPEN TO THE PUBLIC, AND SHOULD YOU VISIT ONE SOMEDAY FOR THE FIRST TIME, BE PREPARED FOR SCENES OF BEAUTY AND SURPRISE.
AMONG THE MOST BEAUTIFUL COMMERCIAL CAVERNS IN THE WORLD ARE THE CAVERNS OF LURAY, IN VIRGINIA. DISCOVERED AUGUST 13, 1878, BY ANDREW CAMPBELL AND BENTON STEBBINS, THESE CAVERNS ARE TODAY THE LARGEST AND MOST POPULAR IN THE EASTERN UNITED STATES.
ALL CAVES OPEN TO THE PUBLIC ARE EQUIPPED FOR THE SAFETY AND CONVENIENCE OF VISITORS. NEVER TRY TO EXPLORE AN UNKNOWN CAVE BY YOURSELF. CAVE EXPLORING, OR "SPELUNKING", AS THE SPORT IS CALLED, CAN BE DANGEROUS.

1966 • Page 79

It Happened THIS MONTH ...EVENTS OUT OF THE PAST

THE McGUFFEY READERS

Among the major forces that were influencing American education, morals, and culture in the West and Midwest from the mid-1800's to the early 1900's were the *McGUFFEY READERS*.

Compiled and edited by *William Holmes McGuffey*, a minister and professor who was born September 23, 1800. The *READERS* sold more than 122,000,000 copies of the original and revised editions.

Each page contained new words, an illustration, a short story, and, on some pages, a few lines of script for practice. The lessons taught kindness, honesty, truthfulness, diligence in study, industry, humility, and modesty.

— K. Lischies '66

It Happened THIS MONTH ...EVENTS OUT OF THE PAST

BOK SINGING TOWER

Among the many tourist attractions to be found in the state of Florida is the *BOK SINGING TOWER*, at Lake Wales. Established by *Edward William Bok*, in honor of his grandparents, the tower is one of the largest *CARILLONS** in existence.

Bok, an American editor and philanthropist, who was born October 9, 1863, brought the idea of the tower over from his native Holland. There such towers have been used as points from which to watch for broken dikes and for enemies. In Florida, the tower is set in the midst of a beautiful bird and animal sanctuary.

*A carillon consists of a set of bells hung in a tower and sounded by pedals, machinery, or by hand. The Singing Tower contains 71 bells, ranging in weight from 11 pounds to 23,000 pounds!

— K. Lischies '66

Among the designs on the tower are the six days of creation, and various Florida plant and animal life.

It Happened THIS MONTH ...EVENTS OUT OF THE PAST — THE MASON JAR

The next time you remove the cap from a Mason jar containing preserves, fruits, or vegetables that your mother or grandmother has canned, remember that closing jars was really a problem in home canning up until about a hundred years ago.

Many inventors were working on the problem at about the same time, and on November 30, 1858, **JOHN L. MASON** patented the closure system which today bears his name.

Housewives used cork (which was scarce and costly), or plugs made from corncobs. On wide-mouthed jars, a layer of wax or lard preserved the contents.

Further refinements to Mason's jar led to widespread canning, and since that time countless families have enjoyed the summer bounties of the garden all through the winter.

HKLISCHIES '66

It Happened THIS MONTH ...EVENTS OUT OF THE PAST — TRAINS – PAST AND FUTURE

FROM AN OLD PRINT

When **THE BEST FRIEND OF CHARLESTON** puffed along at 21 miles an hour on a 6-mile trial track, American *RAILROADING* had begun. After this initial run in December, 1830, regular service was established Christmas Day. The train ran well until June, when the fireman got tired of hearing the hissing of steam from the safety valve. He stopped the noise by tying the valve down. Result–America's first train-boiler explosion.

Although many improvements in rail travel have been made, trains of the future will be quite different from what we know today—they may travel 300 miles an hour in tunnels 500 feet below ground, or ride on cushions of air in sealed tubes at up to 400 miles an hour, powered by turbofan jets.

SOUND FAR-FETCHED? Probably not any more than steam-driven trains did to the early pioneers.

HKLISCHIES '66

1967

Nineteen Sixty-Seven

It Happened THIS MONTH
...EVENTS OUT OF THE PAST

LEAGUE OF NATIONS

(JAN)

The first major organization dedicated to the preservation of peace and international cooperation was the **LEAGUE OF NATIONS**. Formally established January 10, 1920, the League set up its headquarters in Geneva, Switzerland. With the exception of the UNITED STATES and SAUDI ARABIA, all of the considerable nations were at some time members.

Disputes that came before the League were handled with varying degrees of success, but major problems could seldom be settled. This caused the influence of the League to decline until finally, on April 18, 1946, the organization ceased to function.
The work of keeping the peace has now been taken over by the United Nations, as hope and faith continue to be placed in man-made organizations.

KLISCHIES '67

It Happened THIS MONTH
...EVENTS OUT OF THE PAST

THE FOUR CHAPLAINS
INTERFAITH IN ACTION

(FEB)

February 3 has been designated as **FOUR CHAPLAINS MEMORIAL DAY** — it is in honor of four military chaplains who gave their lives so that others might live when their troopship was sunk during World War II.
The chaplains were on the S.S. DORCHESTER, which was part of a convoy bound for Greenland, when an enemy submarine torpedoed the slow-moving ship on the morning of February 3, 1943. Before long, men were out on the deck and dropping into the black, frigid waters. The ship was sinking fast, and there were still many soldiers without life preservers. The chaplains quickly made their decision, and when last seen, just before the crippled ship slipped beneath the icy water, all four were standing on the deck, arms locked, their life preservers given away, each one praying to God.

REMEMBER THESE NAMES —
GEORGE FOX - *PROTESTANT*
CLARK POLING - *PROTESTANT*
JOHN P. WASHINGTON - *CATHOLIC*
ALEXANDER D. GOODE - *JEW*
The selfless, courageous deed of these dedicated men is an inspiration to all who call themselves children of God.

KLISCHIES '67

1967 • Page 85

It Happened THIS MONTH
...EVENTS OUT OF THE PAST

FIRST PLANETARIUM OPENED TO PUBLIC
ADLER PLANETARIUM, CHICAGO, ILLINOIS
MAY 10, 1930

Imagine that you are sitting in a comfortable chair some early evening looking at the sky. As darkness comes on, birds gradually stop their singing and twittering, and soon the sounds of the night are heard — crickets, the hooting of an owl, barking dogs over the hill. You watch a not-quite-full moon rising, pick out familiar stars and constellations, and observe them until a faint red glow in the east tells you that dawn is about to break. As the sky grows brighter, the night sounds fade away. Somewhere a rooster crows, and you know that another day has begun.

HAVE YOU BEEN SITTING UP ALL NIGHT?

NO — you are in a PLANETARIUM, and your 12-hour journey probably took no longer than 30 minutes. A planetarium is a round room with a dome-shaped ceiling. In the center of the floor is the projector, looking like a huge dumbbell on a stand, which can duplicate any sky pattern from the past and of the future. With the addition of appropriate sound effects, the illusion of being outside can be quite convincing.

H K LISCHIES '67

It Happened THIS MONTH
...EVENTS OUT OF THE PAST

FLAG DAY

PATHFINDERS IN THE U.S.A. —
Show your colors...
DISPLAY "OLD GLORY" ON FLAG DAY

June 14 has been designated as FLAG DAY. It was on this date in 1777 that the Continental Congress adopted the "STARS AND STRIPES" as the official flag of the United States. But it wasn't until 1889 that the first PATRIOTIC observance of the day took place.

Today flags are displayed on government and public buildings and by private citizens in and about their homes.

TO PROPERLY DISPLAY YOUR FLAG, CONSULT YOUR LOCAL LIBRARY FOR INFORMATION AND PICTURES.

H K LISCHIES '67

Page 86 • 1967

It Happened THIS MONTH
...EVENTS OUT OF THE PAST

HAPPY BIRTHDAY!

"IT HAPPENED THIS MONTH" BEGAN APPEARING IN THE *GUIDE* TEN YEARS AGO THIS MONTH. HERE ARE SOME OF THE EVENTS WHICH TOOK PLACE THE SAME MONTH THIS FEATURE WAS BORN.

THE SEASON'S FIRST TROPICAL STORM, **HURRICANE AUDREY**, SWEPT IN FROM THE GULF OF MEXICO AND LASHED ACROSS THE STATE OF LOUISIANA — THEN CONTINUED AS FAR NORTH AS OHIO AND PENNSYLVANIA.

EVANGELIST **BILLY GRAHAM** SPOKE TO A RECORD CROWD AT NEW YORK'S YANKEE STADIUM. AT LEAST 100,000 PEOPLE JAMMED THE FAMOUS BALL PARK TO HEAR THE PREACHING OF GOD'S WORD.

FORMER ARMY GENERAL **DWIGHT EISENHOWER** WAS PRESIDENT OF THE UNITED STATES.

NIKITA KHRUSHCHEV WAS PREMIER OF RUSSIA

MANY OF YOU READING THIS WERE ONLY ONE, TWO, OR THREE YEARS OLD WHEN THESE EVENTS TOOK PLACE. IN FACT, SOME OF YOU WEREN'T EVEN BORN YET! SO, HAVE YOUR PARENTS OR AN OLDER BROTHER OR SISTER FILL YOU IN ON THE DETAILS.

HKLISCHIES '67

It Happened THIS MONTH
...EVENTS OUT OF THE PAST

THE SEAL OF THE UNITED STATES

ON THE SAME DAY AS THE SIGNING OF THE *DECLARATION OF INDEPENDENCE*, JULY 4, 1776, THE FOUNDING FATHERS APPOINTED A COMMITTEE COMPOSED OF "DR. FRANKLIN, MR. J. ADAMS AND MR. JEFFERSON" TO DESIGN A SEAL FOR THE NEW NATION.

THE COMMITTEE'S FIRST DESIGNS WERE SUBMITTED AUGUST 20, 1776. ONE DESIGN SHOWED MOSES DIVIDING THE RED SEA AND THE WATERS CLOSING OVER PHARAOH. ANOTHER SHOWED THE CHILDREN OF ISRAEL GUIDED BY THE CLOUD BY DAY AND THE PILLAR OF FIRE BY NIGHT.

BECAUSE THE WAR OF INDEPENDENCE WAS GOING ON AT THIS TIME, CONGRESS SHELVED THE PROJECT. IT WASN'T UNTIL SIX YEARS AND TWO COMMITTEES LATER THAT A DESIGN WAS FINALLY APPROVED.

THE SEAL APPEARS ON OFFICIAL PUBLICATIONS AND STATIONARY, FLAGS AND MONUMENTS. BOTH SIDES (OBVERSE AND REVERSE) OF THE SEAL APPEAR ON THE ONE-DOLLAR BILL. THE FAMOUS MOTTO, E PLURIBUS UNUM, IS LATIN FOR **"OUT OF MANY, ONE."**

HKLISCHIES '67

1968

Nineteen Sixty-Eight

It Happened THIS MONTH
...EVENTS OUT OF THE PAST

PAUL REVERE

BORN JANUARY 1, 1735
ONE WHO CONTRIBUTED MUCH TO THE DEVELOPMENT OF OUR NATION

Mention the name PAUL REVERE, and most people think of Revere's famous MIDNIGHT RIDE through Concord and Lexington warning everyone that the British were coming. But Revere was many other things besides being a PATRIOT. When he was 13 years old, Paul was apprenticed as a silversmith in his father's shop. It was here he learned to make the many beautiful PITCHERS, TRAYS, and other silver items which today are prized possessions.

WHEN THE TOWN'S ONLY DENTIST LEFT, REVERE ADDED DENTISTRY TO HIS ACCOMPLISHMENTS. HE EVEN MADE A SET OF FALSE TEETH FOR GEORGE WASHINGTON.

REVERE LEARNED THE SECRET OF MAKING GUNPOWDER FOR THE CONTINENTAL ARMY.

AFTER THE REVOLUTIONARY WAR, REVERE BEGAN HIS BELLMAKING BUSINESS.

REVERE'S DESIRE TO SEE NEW INDUSTRIES ESTABLISHED IN AMERICA, CAUSED HIM TO OPEN THE FIRST FACTORY TO PRODUCE COPPER SHEETING. A SPECIAL CUSTOMER OF HIS WAS ROBERT FULTON, WHO NEEDED COPPER TO MAKE BOILERS FOR HIS STEAMBOAT.

'68 HKLISCHIES

It Happened THIS MONTH
...EVENTS OUT OF THE PAST

IWO JIMA MEMORIAL

ALSO KNOWN AS THE UNITED STATES MARINE CORPS WAR MEMORIAL

One of the most famous pictures to come out of WORLD WAR II is the one showing the raising of the American flag on MOUNT SURIBACHI, on the island of IWO JIMA, in the Pacific Ocean. This took place February 23, 1945, and included five Marines and a Navy medical corpsman. So impressive was the event, that it has been transformed into a magnificent bronze monument, which is located near Arlington National Cemetery, in Washington, D.C.

THE FIGURES ARE 32 FEET HIGH, AND ARE STANDING ON A PILE OF ROCKS 6 FEET HIGH. ONE RIFLE IS 16 FEET LONG. CANTEENS THE SIZE THESE FIGURES CARRY COULD HOLD 32 QUARTS OF WATER!

Engraved on the base are these words:
"UNCOMMON VALOR WAS A COMMON VIRTUE"

HKLISCHIES '68

It Happened THIS MONTH
...EVENTS OUT OF THE PAST

ANIMALS BECOMING EXTINCT

MARTHA — LAST OF HER SPECIES, DIED AT 1:00 P.M., SEPTEMBER 1, 1914, AGE 29, IN THE CINCINNATI ZOOLOGICAL GARDENS. **EXTINCT**

There is something terribly final when a species of animal becomes extinct. An animal or bird population may number millions or even billions, but when the species dies out it is hard to imagine how such a thing could have happened. **Consider the Passenger Pigeon** — estimated to number between three billion and five billion in the early 1800's, the birds were killed by the thousands for food and for reducing their population. By 1880 it was already too late to save the pigeon. On September 1, 1914, the last of the species died.

THE POLAR BEAR IS AN ANIMAL THAT IS RAPIDLY VANISHING

Today many animals, birds, and fish are on the verge of extinction. Only action and an educated people can save these creatures. Here is a partial list of wildlife in danger of vanishing:

- GRIZZLY BEAR
- MOUNTAIN LION
- FOX SQUIRREL
- WHOOPING CRANE
- GREAT WHITE HERON
- BALD EAGLE (SYMBOL OF THE UNITED STATES)
- ATLANTIC SALMON
- BOWHEAD WHALE
- AMERICAN ALLIGATOR

It Happened THIS MONTH
...EVENTS OUT OF THE PAST

DESMOND DOSS — Medal of Honor Winner

During times of war, many nations honor their fighting men by awarding medals in recognition of some outstanding performance on the battlefield. The *Croix de Guerre* is a well-known medal given by France; in England the *Victoria Cross* and the *Order of the British Empire* are high awards. The highest medal awarded by the United States is the *Congressional Medal of Honor*. To earn this medal, a man must perform a deed of bravery or self-sacrifice "above and beyond the call of duty."

One man who met this requirement is *Corporal Desmond T. Doss*, who was a Seventh-day Adventist medical corpsman during World War Two. Because of Doss's complete dedication to duty, at least 75 wounded soldiers were saved through his own efforts during one particular battle on Okinawa. For this, Corporal Doss was awarded the nation's highest honor October 12, 1945, at ceremonies in Washington, D.C. He is the only conscientious objector so honored during that war.

It Happened THIS MONTH
...EVENTS OUT OF THE PAST
WINSTON CHURCHILL

"I HAVE NOTHING TO OFFER BUT BLOOD, TOIL, TEARS AND SWEAT"

SO SPOKE SIR WINSTON CHURCHILL TO THE BRITISH PEOPLE WHEN HE WAS CALLED UPON TO BE THEIR LEADER, OR PRIME MINISTER, DURING THE EARLY PART OF WORLD WAR II.

CHURCHILL, WHO WAS BORN NOVEMBER 30, 1874, WAS AN OUTSTANDING MAN IN MANY FIELDS; BUT HE IS BEST REMEMBERED AS THE PRIME MINISTER OF ENGLAND DURING THE SECOND WORLD WAR.
AS THE WAR PROGRESSED, LONDON WAS BOMBED DAY AND NIGHT, BUT CHURCHILL'S CONFIDENCE AND COURAGE RANG OUT IN EVERY SPEECH. HE GAVE THE PEOPLE THE WILL AND THE SPIRIT TO CARRY ON DURING THOSE DARK AND TRYING YEARS.

CHURCHILL TOOK UP PAINTING IN 1915, BECOMING A SKILLFUL LANDSCAPE ARTIST. HE PURSUED THIS HOBBY IN THE LAST YEARS OF HIS LIFE.

H. KLISCHIES '68

It Happened THIS MONTH
...EVENTS OUT OF THE PAST
THE QUEEN MARY

QUEEN MARY RETIRES FROM SERVICE

THE QUEEN MARY, ENGLAND'S SYMBOL OF MAJESTY, LUXURY, AND ELEGANT OCEAN TRAVEL, WAS FINALLY RETIRED FROM SERVICE DURING 1967 AFTER HAVING CROSSED THE ATLANTIC OCEAN 1,000 TIMES.

LAUNCHED IN 1934, THE LINER QUICKLY ESTABLISHED A WORLD SPEED RECORD FOR OCEAN CROSSINGS - 3 DAYS, 20 HOURS 42 MINUTES. DURING WORLD WAR II SHE BECAME A TROOP CARRIER, CRAMMING 15,000 SOLDIERS ON BOARD-AN ENTIRE DIVISION! HER FAST SPEED ENABLED HER TO OUTRUN ENEMY SUBMARINES.

THE QUEEN MARY WAS RECENTLY PURCHASED BY THE CITY OF LONG BEACH, CALIFORNIA, AND BECAME PERMANENTLY DOCKED THERE IN DECEMBER, 1967. THE LINER WILL BE USED AS A FLOATING HOTEL, MARITIME MUSEUM, CONVENTION CENTER, AND GENERAL TOURIST ATTRACTION.

1,019 FT.
555 FT.
WASHINGTON MONUMENT — QUEEN MARY

THE SHIP WAS LIKE A FLOATING CITY, CARRYING 2,000 PASSENGERS AND 1,000 CREWMEN. THERE WERE 600 TELEPHONES, 2 RADIO STATIONS AND 378 FIRE HYDRANTS. SHE SERVED 8,000 MEALS A DAY - THE BREAKFAST MENU ALONE HAD 80 ITEMS TO CHOOSE FROM! A FULL-TIME GARDENER TENDED THE 12,000 PLANTS ON BOARD THE SHIP.

H. KLISCHIES '68

1969

Nineteen Sixty-Nine

It Happened THIS MONTH
...EVENTS OUT OF THE PAST
INAUGURATION DAY

Once every four years in November the people of the United States choose their president, but it isn't until the following January 20 that the new president is *INAUGURATED* and assumes the leadership of the country for the coming four-year term.

When Richard M. Nixon is inaugurated this month as the 37th President of the United States, he will be only the sixth to do so in January. Previously, inaugurals were held in March, but this was changed to January in 1933 at the beginning of Franklin D. Roosevelt's first term.

KLISCHIES '69

It Happened THIS MONTH
...EVENTS OUT OF THE PAST
PILGRIM'S PROGRESS

"...A MAN CLOTHED WITH RAGS..., A BOOK IN HIS HAND, AND A GREAT BURDEN ON HIS BACK."

So begins the story of *Christian*, as he leaves the city of *Destruction* and heads for the celestial city of *Zion*. This allegory, written by Englishman *John Bunyan*, and published in February, 1678, is actually an account of every Christian's journey through life. As Christian struggles along, he is hindered by people such as *Mistrust, Hypocrisy,* and *Worldly Wiseman.* But he is also helped by *Goodwill, Watchful, Hopeful,* and *Experience.*

Next to the Bible, *Pilgrim's Progress* is probably the greatest religious book. You can get a condensed version of the book at your public library.

It Happened THIS MONTH
...EVENTS OUT OF THE PAST

FIRST SUCCESSFUL EARTH ORBIT

FLYING AROUND IN OUTER SPACE IS A RELATIVELY NEW VENTURE. IN FACT, THE FIRST SUCCESSFUL **MANNED ORBIT** AROUND THE WORLD TOOK PLACE JUST *EIGHT* YEARS AGO, WHEN SOME OF YOU JUNIORS WERE ONLY TWO OR THREE YEARS OLD.

IT WAS ON APRIL 12, 1961, THAT SOVIET RUSSIA SENT ITS SPACEMAN, **YURI GAGARIN**, ON HIS HISTORIC SPACE JOURNEY. SINCE THEN, OTHER FLIGHTS BY BOTH RUSSIA AND THE UNITED STATES HAVE BEEN MADE, PUSHING DEEPER INTO SPACE.

MAN IS REACHING OUT FOR THE PLANETS. PLANS ARE BEING MADE TO EXPLORE THIS SOLAR SYSTEM. WILL MAN BE ALLOWED TO DO IT?

INSIDE A SOVIET SPACE CAPSULE, AS RECONSTRUCTED FROM AVAILABLE INFORMATION

It Happened THIS MONTH
...EVENTS OUT OF THE PAST

LEAGUE OF AMERICAN WHEELMEN

DURING THE EARLY DAYS OF CYCLING, AN ORGANIZATION CALLED THE **LEAGUE OF AMERICAN WHEELMEN** WAS FORMED, WHICH PLAYED AN IMPORTANT PART IN PROMOTING *BICYCLING* IN AMERICA. ORGANIZED MAY 30, 1880, THE L.A.W. (AS THE LEAGUE WAS COMMONLY CALLED) FOUGHT FOR THE RIGHT OF WHEELMEN TO USE PUBLIC STREETS, HIGHWAYS, AND PARKS.

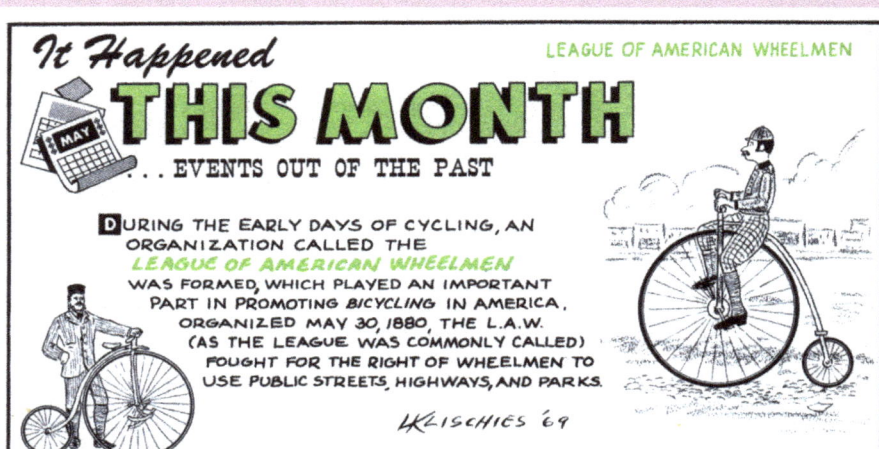

THE L.A.W. ENCOURAGED TOURING, AND SOON PEOPLE WERE TRAVELING INTO STRANGE PARTS OF THE COUNTRY, SENDING, OR BRINGING BACK INFORMATION ABOUT ROAD CONDITIONS, HOTELS, SIGHTS TO SEE, AND SO ON.

CYCLING GREW IN POPULARITY UNTIL DISASTER STRUCK IN 1898. A STRANGE CONTRAPTION CALLED THE "*AUTOMOBILE*" APPEARED, AND IT DIDN'T TAKE PEOPLE LONG TO GIVE UP THEIR BIKES AND ADOPT THE "HORSELESS CARRIAGE."

But...AS YOU LOOK AROUND TODAY, YOU CAN SEE THAT PEOPLE ARE ONCE AGAIN DISCOVERING THE DELIGHTS OF CYCLING. AND, IT'S ESPECIALLY FUN WHEN THE FAMILY CAN DO IT TOGETHER!

It Happened THIS MONTH
...EVENTS OUT OF THE PAST

TREATY OF VERSAILLES

THIS MONTH MARKS THE 50TH ANNIVERSARY OF THE SIGNING OF THE *TREATY OF VERSAILLES*, ENDING WORLD WAR I.

AFTER FOUR YEARS OF WAR, WITH ITS TERRIBLE DESTRUCTION AND LOSS OF LIFE, THE ALLIES RENDERED GERMANY POWERLESS BY NOVEMBER, 1918. A PEACE CONFERENCE CONVENED IN PARIS, DECEMBER, 1918, BUT IT WASN'T UNTIL JUNE 28, 1919, THAT THE PEACE TREATY WAS SIGNED.

THE MAGNIFICENT **HALL OF MIRRORS** IN WHICH THE TREATY WAS SIGNED

HKLISCHIES '69

It Happened THIS MONTH
...EVENTS OUT OF THE PAST

WEDGWOOD POTTERY

ORIGINATED BY *JOSIAH WEDGWOOD*, AN ENGLISH POTTER, WHO WAS CHRISTENED JULY 12, 1730

EVEN THOUGH YOU ARE FORTUNATE TO HAVE SOME WEDGWOOD POTTERY IN YOUR HOME YOU MAY NOT HAVE REALIZED THAT THE ORIGINATOR OF THIS FINE POTTERY, *JOSIAH WEDGWOOD*, STARTED HIS CAREER WITH SEVERAL HANDICAPS. WHEN HE WAS ALMOST 12 YEARS OLD, JOSIAH HAD SMALLPOX, WHICH LEFT HIS FACE DEEPLY POCK-MARKED. THE DISEASE ALSO SETTLED IN HIS KNEE, MAKING HIM LAME. TWO GOOD LEGS WERE NEEDED TO OPERATE THE POTTER'S WHEEL—JOSIAH MANAGED WITH ONE. BUT HE DID SUCCEED, AND TODAY HIS BEAUTIFUL PIECES ARE COLLECTED BY LOVERS OF FINE POTTERY.

THE PORTLAND VASE MADE OF DEEP-BLUE GLASS, ON WHICH A LAYER OF OPAQUE WHITE GLASS WAS APPLIED. THE FIGURES ARE CARVED FROM THIS LAYER OF GLASS.

BY HIS SKILL AND TASTE, WEDGWOOD MADE THE POTTER'S CRAFT ONE OF THE IMPORTANT INDUSTRIES OF ENGLAND.

HKLISCHIES '69

It Happened THIS MONTH
...EVENTS OUT OF THE PAST

SWIMMING THE ENGLISH CHANNEL

Competition in sports can bring about almost any kind of contest. In swimming, the challenge has been to cross the body of water between France and England, known as the **ENGLISH CHANNEL**, in the shortest time. The first woman to accomplish the crossing was **GERTRUDE EDERLE**. She broke the existing record when she swam from France to England on August 6, 1926, in 14 hours 31 minutes. Her record was to stand for 24 years.

THE DISTANCE BETWEEN DOVER AND CAPE GRIS-NEZ IS ABOUT 22 MILES

IN AUGUST, 1950, **FLORENCE CHADWICK** BROKE THE RECORD, CROSSING IN 13 HOURS 20 MINUTES. THE FOLLOWING YEAR SHE SWAM FROM ENGLAND TO FRANCE, BECOMING THE FIRST WOMAN TO SWIM THE CHANNEL BOTH WAYS.

H KLISCHIES '69

It Happened THIS MONTH
...EVENTS OUT OF THE PAST

JOHNNY APPLESEED

The next time you're munching on an apple the name **JOHNNY APPLESEED** may come to mind. So much legend has grown up around this actual frontier character of almost 200 years ago that some people think he never existed. His real name was **JOHN CHAPMAN**, and he was born September 26, 1774, in Leominster, Massachusetts. Chapman is best known for his apple-planting activities in and around Pennsylvania, Ohio, Illinois, and Indiana. He would clear an area in a forest, plant his apple seeds, then move on to another part of the wilderness, and repeat this process. Later, when the settlers came in, they would find apple trees already blooming for them.

CHAPMAN NEVER MARRIED OR HAD A HOME OF HIS OWN, BUT STAYED WITH FRONTIER SETTLERS, OR OUT IN THE WOODS

HERB KLISCHIES, SR. '69

APPLES ARE GOOD FOR YOU - HAVE AT LEAST ONE A DAY!

JONATHAN • WINESAP • DELICIOUS • GRIMES GOLDEN • BALDWIN • NORTHERN SPY • ROME BEAUTY

1969 • Page 103

It Happened THIS MONTH
...EVENTS OUT OF THE PAST

THE PLEDGE OF ALLEGIANCE

"I GIVE MY HEART AND MY HAND TO MY COUNTRY, ONE COUNTRY, ONE LANGUAGE, ONE FLAG"

HAD YOU BEEN SALUTING THE AMERICAN FLAG AROUND 1892 OR EARLIER, YOU WOULD HAVE REPEATED THE ABOVE, KNOWN AS THE "BALCH" SALUTE. AT LEAST ONE MAN WHO LIVED AT THAT TIME, **FRANCIS BELLAMY**, OF ROME, NEW YORK, FELT THE SALUTE TO BE CHILDISH AND LACKING IN DIGNITY. SO IT WAS, THAT WHEN THE 400TH ANNIVERSARY OF THE DISCOVERY OF AMERICA WAS BEING PLANNED, WITH APPROPRIATE FLAG-RAISING CEREMONIES ON OCTOBER 12, 1892, BELLAMY DECIDED TO REWRITE THE PLEDGE.

THIS IS THE ORIGINAL PLEDGE OF ALLEGIANCE AS WRITTEN BY FRANCIS BELLAMY:

I PLEDGE ALLEGIANCE TO MY FLAG AND (TO) THE REPUBLIC FOR WHICH IT STANDS — ONE NATION INDIVISIBLE — WITH LIBERTY AND JUSTICE FOR ALL.

IN 1923 "MY FLAG" WAS CHANGED TO "THE FLAG OF THE UNITED STATES." "OF AMERICA WAS ADDED IN 1924, AND "UNDER GOD" ADDED IN 1954.

HERB KLISCHIES, SR. '69

It Happened THIS MONTH
...EVENTS OUT OF THE PAST

THE LOUVRE

TO SEE THE GREATEST ART COLLECTION IN THE WORLD, YOU WOULD HAVE TO GO TO PARIS, FRANCE. THERE YOU WOULD FIND THE **LOUVRE** (Pronounced LOO-vruh), THE WORLD'S LARGEST PALACE, WITH ITS SEVEN MUSEUMS, CONTAINING MANY PRICELESS ART TREASURES.

THE *LOUVRE* WAS ORIGINALLY OPENED TO THE PUBLIC ON A TEMPORARY BASIS IN AUGUST, 1793, CLOSING AT THE END OF SEPTEMBER. IT WAS REOPENED ON A PERMANENT BASIS IN NOVEMBER, 1793.

HERB KLISCHIES, SR. '69

THE ART MUSEUM CONTAINS LEONARDO DA VINCI'S *MONA LISA*. IN THE SCULPTURE MUSEUM IS THE FAMOUS ANCIENT GREEK STATUE OF *VENUS DE MILO*.

1970

Nineteen Seventy

It Happened THIS MONTH
...EVENTS OUT OF THE PAST

THE FOUR FREEDOMS

During the dark days just before the complete outbreak of World War II, freedom had just about been extinguished within the conquered parts of Europe and Asia. In his annual *State of the Union* message to Congress, given January 6, 1941, United States President Franklin D. Roosevelt said: "We look forward to a world founded upon four essential human freedoms." These became known as **THE FOUR FREEDOMS**.

World War II came to an end, and today, 25 years later, President Roosevelt's world of the Four Freedoms has not yet become a reality.

— HERB KLISCHIES, SR. '70

It Happened THIS MONTH
...EVENTS OUT OF THE PAST

EMMA WILLARD - *Pioneer Educator*

BORN FEBRUARY 23, 1787

A young lady of the early 1800's, looking through the "Help Wanted" section of her newspaper, would never find such a selection of job openings for women as this ➡. The attitude of the people kept the average girl from getting any further education beyond the basic reading, writing, and arithmetic. Many people felt it was contrary to the will of God, unladylike, and even *physically harmful* for a woman to study mathematics and science!

It was **EMMA WILLARD**, a young schoolteacher living in Connecticut, who changed the idea of education in the United States by establishing a college just for girls. Mrs. Willard was criticized and ridiculed but she stands out today as the pioneer educator of American women.

— HERB KLISCHIES, SR. '70

It Happened THIS MONTH
...EVENTS OUT OF THE PAST

ADHESIVE POSTAGE STAMPS

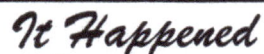

Are you a PHILATELIST?

YOU ARE IF YOU COLLECT *POSTAGE STAMPS*. AND BY COLLECTING THESE SMALL RECTANGULAR PIECES OF PAPER, YOU WILL BE ABLE TO FOLLOW THE EVENTS OF HISTORY FROM THE DAYS OF CHRISTOPHER COLUMBUS TO THOSE OF OUTER SPACE.

THE ADOPTION OF *ADHESIVE POSTAGE STAMPS* ON MARCH 3, 1847, WAS AN IMPORTANT IMPROVEMENT IN THE HISTORY OF THE UNITED STATES POSTAL SERVICE.

ONE OF THE FIRST UNITED STATES STAMPS ISSUED WITH GLUE ON THE BACK (1847)

IF YOU WANT TO SEE SOME OF THE GOOD AND BEAUTIFUL THAT MAN HAS DONE, START A STAMP COLLECTION. CHECK THE "PEN PALS" SECTION OF THE GUIDE FOR JUNIORS WANTING TO TRADE STAMPS.

Some of the many interesting things you'll find on these tiny Storybooks...

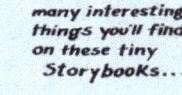     

UNITED STATES-CANADA FRIENDSHIP BRIDGE 1948 | 50TH ANNIVERSARY OF THE RED CROSS 1931 | MAGNOLIA-STATE FLOWER OF MISSISSIPPI 1967 | "WIN THE WAR" 1943

KLISCHIES, SR. '70

It Happened THIS MONTH
...EVENTS OUT OF THE PAST

JOHN MUIR - *Father of our National Parks*

Born April 21, 1838

DEDICATED TO SAVING GOD'S WILDERNESS

THE NEXT TIME YOU'RE IN ONE OF AMERICA'S GREAT NATIONAL PARKS, REMEMBER THE NAME **JOHN MUIR**. FROM SCOTLAND JOHN MUIR CAME TO AMERICA WHEN HE WAS 11 YEARS OLD. AS A YOUNG MAN HE ROAMED THROUGH AMERICA'S WILDERNESS. ONE SUMMER HE WENT ON A 1000-MILE HIKE! THESE WANDERINGS BECAME THE FOUNDATION OF HIS FUTURE WORK— *THE PRESERVATION OF AMERICA'S WILDERNESS.* THROUGH ARTICLES AND SPEECHES, MUIR AROUSED THE NATION TO SAVE ITS GREAT MOUNTAINS AND FORESTS.

IT IS BECAUSE OF THE FORESIGHT OF MEN SUCH AS JOHN MUIR THAT WE TODAY MAY ENJOY VAST REGIONS OF UNSPOILED WOODLAND.

HERB KLISCHIES, SR. '70

It Happened THIS MONTH
...EVENTS OUT OF THE PAST

JOAN OF ARC
BURNED AT THE STAKE
MAY 30, 1431
ROUEN, FRANCE

Mention the name JOAN OF ARC and many people will think only of a young girl who was tried as a witch and burned at the stake. Actually Joan did much for her native France. When she was 17 years old, Joan, wearing a suit of white armor and listening to her "VOICES," led the French army to several victories over France's enemy, England. During one of these battles Joan was captured.

At Joan's trial 40 theologians, monks, and friars, presided over by BISHOP PIERRE CAUCHON, found her guilty of a dozen crimes, including heresy, blasphemy, and idolatry, and condemned her to die at the stake.

Twenty-five years later a new court decided Joan was innocent of all charges. On May 16, 1920, the Catholic Church declared her a Saint.

HERB KLISCHIES, SR. '70

It Happened THIS MONTH
...EVENTS OUT OF THE PAST

THE BATTLE OF WATERLOO

Many decisive battles are recorded in world history. One such battle took place June 18, 1815, at a place called WATERLOO, in Belgium.

Napoleon Bonaparte was sweeping the French army across Europe. The English and Dutch under Wellington took up a position at Waterloo, waiting for Napoleon to attack. Having won many other victories, Napoleon, the greatest conqueror of modern times, boasted that the fighting at Waterloo would be a French picnic.

The battle began at 11:30 A.M. and was fought with great fury. At about 6:00 P.M. Blücher arrived with an army of Prussians, and by dark the battle was over. Almost 90,000 men from both sides had been either killed or wounded. Many thousands of horses had also died. The French army was almost entirely destroyed. Gone also were all plans Napoleon had had for conquering all of Europe.

TODAY, THE WORD WATERLOO HAS BECOME A SYMBOL FOR DEFEAT.

It Happened THIS MONTH
...EVENTS OUT OF THE PAST

IGNACE PADEREWSKI
COMPOSER
MUSICIAN
PATRIOT
STATESMAN
HUMANITARIAN
BORN NOVEMBER 6, 1860

Look at any list of the great men of Poland and you'll always find the name of pianist **IGNACE PADEREWSKI**. By the time he was four years old Paderewski was already playing the piano with both hands. He became a concert pianist giving recitals all over the world. Although an accomplished musician, Paderewski would still practice many hours before each concert.

One day while practicing a Chopin étude, Paderewski noticed a spider hanging over the piano. When he played another piece, the spider retreated to the ceiling. The étude brought him down. Another tune made him retreat again— the étude brought him down again. Paderewski was able to play for his "friend" in this manner for many weeks, the spider always coming down when he "heard" that Chopin étude.

HERB KLISCHIES SR. '70

It Happened THIS MONTH
...EVENTS OUT OF THE PAST

WESTMINSTER ABBEY

One of the most impressive buildings in London, England, is **WESTMINSTER ABBEY**.

Dedicated December 30, 1065, it has been enlarged and altered many times since. Here the kings and queens of England since 1066 have been crowned. The Coronation Chair— where the new king sits to be crowned— rests on the **STONE OF DESTINY**, a flat rock on which Scottish kings were once crowned. This is to remind Scotsmen that England's king is king of Scotland, too.

Kings, statesmen, and other important people are buried in the Abbey, including the great missionary— **DAVID LIVINGSTONE**.

HERB KLISCHIES SR. '70

1971

Nineteen Seventy-One

1971 • Page 115

It Happened THIS MONTH
...EVENTS OUT OF THE PAST

QUEEN VICTORIA
"QUEEN OF THE UNITED KINGDOM OF GREAT BRITIAN AND IRELAND, AND EMPRESS OF INDIA"

ONE OF THE GREATEST RULERS IN ENGLISH HISTORY WAS **QUEEN VICTORIA.** COMING TO THE THRONE WHEN SHE WAS ONLY 18 YEARS OLD, VICTORIA RULED FOR 63 YEARS, THE LONGEST REIGN OF ANY BRITISH MONARCH.

THE VICTORIAN ERA, NAMED FOR HER, WAS A TIME IN WHICH GREAT BRITIAN REACHED THE HEIGHT OF ITS POWER — A PERIOD OF GREAT INDUSTRIAL EXPANSION.

QUEEN VICTORIA'S DEATH JANUARY 22, 1901, MARKED THE END OF AN ERA.

HERB KLISCHIES SR.
'71

It Happened THIS MONTH
...EVENTS OUT OF THE PAST

FRANCISCO VASQUEZ de CORONADO

THUNDERING OUT OF THE COUNTRY OF MEXICO DURING FEBRUARY, 1541, AND INTO THE SOUTHWESTERN UNITED STATES CAME THE SPANISH GENERAL *CORONADO,* IN SEARCH OF RICH GOLDEN CITIES AND WEALTHY LANDS OF GOLD, SILVER, AND JEWELS.

GOING AS FAR AS KANSAS AND FINDING ONLY POOR, SIMPLE INDIAN TRIBES, CORONADO RETURNED TO MEXICO IN DISGRACE AND DIED SOON AFTER.

BUT... CORONADO'S VENTURE INTO KANSAS LEFT ITS MARK, FOR HE INTRODUCED THE HORSE TO THE PLAINS. FROM THAT TIME ON THE LIVES OF THE INDIANS WERE NEVER QUITE THE SAME SINCE THEY NOW HAD GREAT **MOBILITY.**

HERB KLISCHIES SR.
'71

It Happened THIS MONTH ...EVENTS OUT OF THE PAST

HAWAII'S FIRST KING — KAMEHAMEHA THE GREAT

At one time the *state* of *Hawaii* was known as the *Kingdom* of Hawaii. After the visit and death of Captain *James Cook*, the Hawaiian Islands underwent 10 years of civil war among its several rulers. *Kamehameha* emerged victorious and was the first to unite the islands under a single ruler.

— *Herb Klisches '72*

Kamehameha is often referred to as the "Father of his Country" because of the positive way in which he ruled Hawaii. June 11 is known as **KAMEHAMEHA DAY**, on which the birthday of Hawaii's first King is celebrated.

It Happened THIS MONTH ...EVENTS OUT OF THE PAST

ROCHAMBEAU — JEAN BAPTISTE DONATIEN de VIMEUR ROCHAMBEAU — BORN JULY 1, 1725

In the American struggle for *Independence*, the ill-fed, ill-equipped army of General *George Washington* was hardly any match for the greatly superior British forces. Recognizing this inadequacy, and hoping to hurt the British, the French government decided to aid the Americans.

In July, 1780, a force of 6,000 Frenchmen, commanded by General *Rochambeau*, landed in Rhode Island. The following year American and French troops laid seige to the British under Maj. Gen. *Charles Cornwallis* at Yorktown, Virginia. On October 19 Cornwallis surrendered.

To Washington and Rochambeau, Yorktown was merely a victory in a well-planned military campaign. Being so close to the war, they did not see that it was actually the grand climax of the American Revolution.

Had Washington not been supplied with French ships, men, and money he would probably have been defeated, and that would have changed the course of American history.

— *Herb Klischies Sr. '71*

It Happened THIS MONTH
...EVENTS OUT OF THE PAST

PIERRE CHARLES L'ENFANT
PLANNER OF THE CITY OF WASHINGTON, D.C.
BORN AUGUST 2, 1754

THE CAPITAL OF THE UNITED STATES HAD BEEN LOCATED IN SEVERAL DIFFERENT CITIES UNTIL 1791, WHEN *PRESIDENT GEORGE WASHINGTON* CHOSE A SECTION OF LAND BETWEEN MARYLAND AND VIRGINIA THAT WAS TO BECOME THE PERMANENT HOME OF THE GOVERNMENT.

WHILE IN PHILADELPHIA, PRESIDENT WASHINGTON HAD RECEIVED AN OFFER FROM FRENCH ARCHITECT *PIERRE CHARLES L'ENFANT* TO LAY OUT PLANS FOR THE NEW FEDERAL CITY.

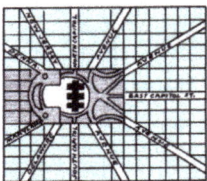

L'ENFANT'S PLAN INCLUDED BROAD, TREE-LINED AVENUES, MALLS, AND OPEN SPACES. ALTHOUGH CHANGES TO THE PLAN HAVE BEEN MADE THROUGH THE YEARS, THE ORIGINAL BASIC LAYOUT IS STILL CREDITED TO L'ENFANT.

ONE OF THE STREETS FORMING THE BOUNDARY LINES OF WASHINGTON IS EASTERN AVENUE. ON THIS STREET YOU'LL FIND THE GENERAL CONFERENCE AND REVIEW AND HERALD BUILDINGS - AND YOUR OWN **GUIDE** OFFICE!

HERB KLISCHIES SR. '71

It Happened THIS MONTH U.S.
...EVENTS OUT OF THE PAST

"UNCLE SAM"

TO MANY PEOPLE IT STILL COMES AS A SURPRISE THAT *"UNCLE SAM"* - THE SYMBOL FOR THE UNITED STATES - WAS A REAL PERSON.

SAMUEL WILSON WAS BORN SEPTEMBER 13, 1766, IN WHAT IS NOW ARLINGTON, MASSACHUSETTS. DURING THE WAR OF 1812, SAM, ALONG WITH HIS BROTHER, SUPPLIED MEAT TO THE ARMY. IN SHIPPING THE MEAT, THE BARRELS WERE STAMPED WITH THE LETTERS *"U.S."*, MEANING *UNITED STATES*. WHEN SOMEONE ASKED THE MEANING OF THE LETTERS, HE WAS JOKINGLY TOLD IT STOOD FOR *"UNCLE SAM"* WILSON.

THE WORD QUICKLY SPREAD AMONG THE SOLDIERS THAT UNCLE SAM WAS CARING FOR THEM. SOON ALL GOVERNMENT PROPERTY BECAME UNCLE SAM'S - WAGONS, WEAPONS, CLOTHING, ETCETERA. AND SO A LEGEND WAS BORN.

THE ORIGINAL UNCLE SAM DIDN'T LOOK LIKE THIS AT ALL. HE HAS UNDERGONE MANY CHANGES BY NEWSPAPER CARTOONISTS.

THANKS TO / SUSAN AIME, NAMPA, IDAHO

HERB KLISCHIES, SR. '71

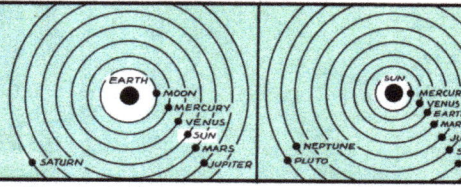

1972

Nineteen Seventy-Two

It Happened THIS MONTH
...EVENTS OUT OF THE PAST

GOLD DISCOVERED!
JANUARY 24, 1848
SUTTER'S MILL
CALIFORNIA

GOLD WAS THE MOST PRECIOUS METAL IN THE GREAT IMAGE OF DANIEL 2

THOUSANDS OF YEARS AGO KING SOLOMON USED GOLD IN HIS TEMPLE, THE EGYPTIANS MADE IDOLS AND OFFERINGS TO PLEASE THEIR 2,000 GODS, AND SUNWORSHIPPERS THOUGHT GOLD TO BE THE SWEAT OF THE SUN. WHENEVER GOLD WAS MENTIONED, MEN WOULD GO SEARCHING FOR IT. SO IT WAS, THAT WHEN JAMES W. MARSHALL DISCOVERED GOLD AT SUTTER'S MILL, "GOLD FEVER" STRUCK AGAIN.

LOCAL PEOPLE CAME BY THE THOUSANDS TO SUTTER'S RANCH. THEY DUG UP HIS GROUND, CAMPED IN HIS BUILDINGS, AND USED HIS CATTLE FOR FOOD. SUTTER COULD GET NO ONE TO FINISH BUILDING HIS MILL OR HARVEST HIS CROPS. BY THE FOLLOWING YEAR, THE NATIONWIDE GOLD RUSH WAS ON.

THE GOLDEN IMAGE OF THE EGYPTIAN KING TUTANKHAMON FORMS THE LID OF HIS COFFIN.

GOLD IS SOMETIMES FOUND IN LUMPS LIKE THIS CALLED NUGGETS

Thanks to STANLEY MAXWELL BERRIEN SPRINGS, MICH.

HERB KLISCHIES '72

It Happened THIS MONTH
...EVENTS OUT OF THE PAST

GIAMBATTISTA BODONI
ITALIAN TYPE FACE DESIGNER
BORN FEBRUARY 26, 1740

EVERY WORD THAT YOU READ IN BOOKS, MAGAZINES, AND NEWSPAPERS IS PRINTED IN A PARTICULAR TYPE "FACE" OR STYLE. EACH FACE HAS A NAME. SOMETIMES THE TYPE IS NAMED AFTER THE PERSON WHO DESIGNED IT. SUCH A TYPE DESIGNER WAS **GIAMBATTISTA BODONI.**

BODONI'S MANY TYPE STYLES ARE AN IMPORTANT ADDITION TO THE FIELD OF PRINTING. HERE IS A SAMPLE OF ONE OF HIS MOST POPULAR FACES -

Bodoni Bold
1234567890

SOME OTHER TYPE SAMPLES (NOT BODONI'S)
OLD English CASlon
Commercial Script
COOper Black FUTURA BOLD
CENtury Schoolbook

LOOK THROUGH THIS ISSUE OF GUIDE AND NOTICE THE DIFFERENT TYPE STYLES USED.

HERB KLISCHIES, SR. '72

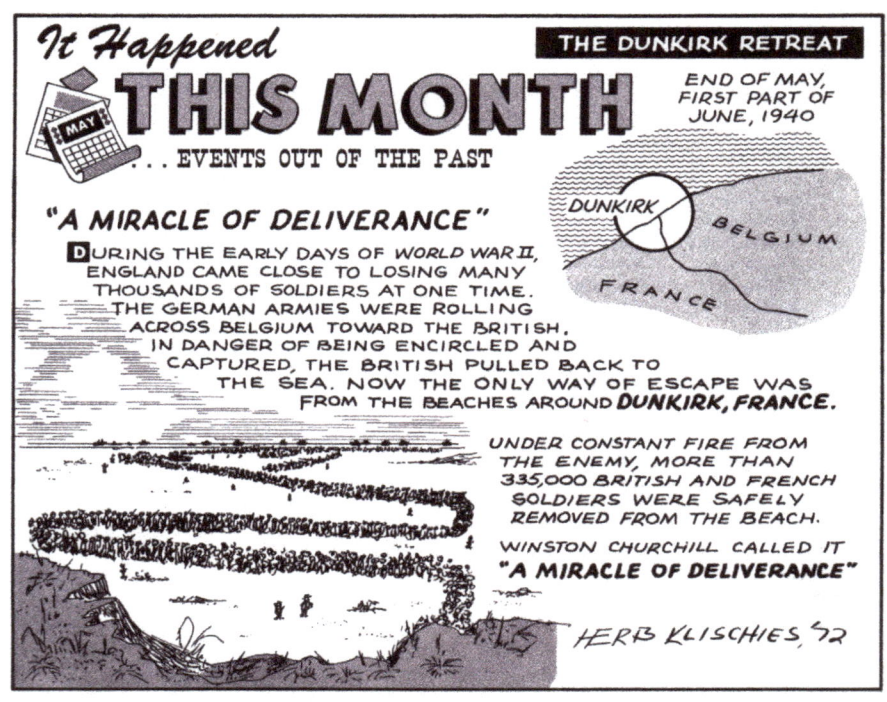

1973

Nineteen Seventy-Three

Page 134 • 1973

It Happened THIS MONTH
...EVENTS OUT OF THE PAST

POMPEII / MOUNT VESUVIUS

Have you ever been close to danger without realizing it until later? The people who lived in the city of **POMPEII**, Italy, only a mile from the foot of **MOUNT VESUVIUS**, found themselves in such a situation. Vesuvius had been quiet for almost 700 years, and people had built many fine homes near the mountain, saying the volcano was extinct.

A SURPRISINGLY MODERN BRONZE BATHTUB DUG FROM THE RUINS

RUINS OF POMPEII, WITH MOUNT VESUVIUS IN BACKGROUND

BUT... on August 24, in the year A.D. 79, a rain of volcanic ash began that lasted for 3 days, at the end of which Pompeii was completely buried, and stayed that way for nearly 17 centuries.

Since its discovery in 1748, more than half of Pompeii has been uncovered, revealing a once-prosperous city of temples, theaters, and two-story houses.

HERB KLISCHIES '73

A MIRROR MADE FROM POLISHED METAL

It Happened THIS MONTH
...EVENTS OUT OF THE PAST

THOMAS NAST
AMERICAN ILLUSTRATOR AND CARTOONIST

Mention the two main political parties in the United States, and two symbols come to mind – the Republican **ELEPHANT**, and the Democratic **DONKEY**. The Democratic Donkey was popularized and the Republican Elephant was originated by political cartoonist **THOMAS NAST**.

PUBLISHED IN 1870

HERB KLISCHIES '73
PUBLISHED IN 1874

Nast, who was born September 27, 1840, in Bavaria, Germany, began working on a newspaper when he was 15. During the Civil War he did many drawings that influenced public opinion in favor of the North.

*Thanks and a HAPPY BIRTHDAY TO KAREN KLISCHIES ORLANDO, FLA.

1974

Nineteen Seventy-Four

1974 • Page 139

It Happened THIS MONTH
...EVENTS OUT OF THE PAST

BURMA BECOMES INDEPENDENT

You probably first heard about the country of **BURMA** from the many stories written by Elder Eric B. Hare, who was a missionary there. Burma was once a part of the British Empire, but became an independent nation January 4, 1948.

Burma is a country of heavy rains, heat, elephants, water buffaloes, rice fields, and pagodas.

Happy Anniversary TO THE PATHFINDERS! 25 Years

BECOME A PATHFINDER AND JOIN IN THE FUN!

SHWE DAGON PAGODA AT RANGOON

HERB KLISCHIES '74

It Happened THIS MONTH
...EVENTS OUT OF THE PAST

THADDEUS KOSCIUSKO

POLISH PATRIOT BORN FEB. 12, 1746

The country of *Poland* has given many great men and women to the world. One such man was the Polish patriot **THADDEUS KOSCIUSKO**, who aided the American colonies during the *Revolutionary War*. Kosciusko's engineering knowledge was of great help in building defenses and fortifications against the British. His most notable fortification was at **WEST POINT**, on the Hudson River, in New York.

"HE WAS IDOLIZED BY THE SOLDIERS FOR HIS BRAVERY...AND BELOVED... FOR THE GOODNESS OF HIS HEART, AND THE GREAT QUALITIES OF HIS MIND..."
— WILLIAM HENRY HARRISON
9th UNITED STATES PRESIDENT

HERB KLISCHIES '74

It Happened THIS MONTH
...EVENTS OUT OF THE PAST

LUTHER BURBANK — "THE PLANT WIZARD" — BORN MARCH 7, 1849, LANCASTER, MASSACHUSETTS

Have you ever eaten a **PLUMCOT**,* or a **POMATO**,* or a **"WHITE" BLACKBERRY**?* Have you ever seen a cactus without spines? These and many other plants are the results of thousands of experiments carried out by **LUTHER BURBANK**.

Burbank devoted his life to creating new trees, flowers, fruits, vegetables, grains, and grasses. His first experiment produced the **BURBANK POTATO** — a large and firm potato.

The **SHASTA DAISY** (right) resulted from crossing the English daisy, the wild American daisy, and their pure white Japanese cousin.

Burbank's desire was to improve every plant that he grew.

*PLUMCOT - CROSSING A PLUM AND AN APRICOT.
POMATO - A FRUIT WHICH GROWS ON A POTATO VINE BUT LOOKS LIKE A SMALL TOMATO.
"WHITE" BLACKBERRY - SO TRANSPARENT YOU CAN SEE THE SEEDS INSIDE.

HERB KLISCHES '74

It Happened THIS MONTH
...EVENTS OUT OF THE PAST

QUEEN ISABELLA I (SPAIN) — BORN APRIL 22, 1451

The discovery of America by Christopher Columbus would not have taken place when it did had it not been for the foresight and support of **QUEEN ISABELLA I** of Spain.

Isabella was one of the few persons who had faith in the plan of Columbus to find a shorter route to the Indies by sailing west.

By giving its support to Columbus, Spain was able to get the first foothold in America, leading to the growth of the Spanish Empire in the **NEW WORLD**.

HERB KLISCHES '74

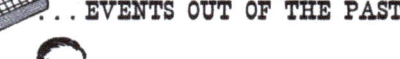

It Happened THIS MONTH
...EVENTS OUT OF THE PAST

ADVENTIST WORLD MISSIONS

1874 / 1974

CENTENNIAL OF ADVENTIST WORLD MISSIONS

ON SEPTEMBER 15, 1874, **JOHN NEVINS ANDREWS**, ALONG WITH HIS TWO CHILDREN, SAILED FROM BOSTON HARBOR, BOUND FOR SWITZERLAND AS THE FIRST OVERSEAS AMBASSADOR OF THE SEVENTH-DAY ADVENTIST CHURCH. LITTLE DID ANDREWS REALIZE HOW MANY HUNDREDS OF TIMES THAT SCENE WOULD BE REPEATED AS DEDICATED MEN AND WOMEN LEAVE THEIR HOMELAND TO CARRY THE GOSPEL MESSAGE TO THE FOUR CORNERS OF THE GLOBE.

THE CHURCH HAS ESTABLISHED ITSELF IN NEARLY 200 OF THE WORLD'S 225 COUNTRIES. THE DIVINE COMMAND WILL SOON BE COMPLETED:

"Go ye into all the world, And teach all nations"

HERB KLISCHES '74

It Happened THIS MONTH
...EVENTS OUT OF THE PAST

ERIE CANAL OPENED

FIRST BOAT TO MAKE ENTIRE TRIP
OCTOBER 26, 1825

WHEN MAN NEEDS A WATERWAY WHERE NATURE HAS FAILED TO PROVIDE ONE, HE BUILDS AN ARTIFICIAL ONE CALLED A **CANAL**.
CANALS ARE USE TO CONNECT BODIES OF WATER - RIVERS TO RIVERS - RIVERS TO LAKES - LAKES TO SEAS. A CANAL'S MAIN PURPOSE IS TO TRANSPORT GOODS AND PEOPLE FROM ONE AREA TO ANOTHER.

THE **ERIE CANAL** IN NEW YORK STATE IS AN EXAMPLE OF HOW A CANAL CAN BENEFIT PEOPLE. TOWNS GREW UP ALONG ITS ROUTE, GROWING IN IMPORTANCE AND POPULATION. THE MAP SHOWS THE ROUTE FROM THE GREAT LAKES TO THE ATLANTIC OCEAN.

SOME Important Canals OF THE WORLD
PANAMA - PANAMA: CONNECTS ATLANTIC AND PACIFIC OCEANS
KIEL - GERMANY: CONNECTS THE BALTIC AND NORTH SEAS
LANGUEDOC - FRANCE: CONNECTS BAY OF BISCAY AND MEDITERRANEAN SEA

IN THE EARLY DAYS CANAL TRAVEL WAS A SLOW BUT BEAUTIFUL JOURNEY. HORSES PULLED THE HEAVY BOATS.

HERB KLISCHIES '74

1975

Nineteen Seventy-Five

It Happened THIS MONTH
...EVENTS OUT OF THE PAST

MOHS HARDNESS SCALE — DEVISED BY FRIEDRICH MOHS, BORN JANUARY 29, 1773

Anyone who has ever tumbled or cut rocks as a hobby has come across the **MOHS SCALE OF HARDNESS**.*

This is named after a German mineralogist, Friedrich Mohs, who devised the scale. Years ago miners would scratch one mineral with another to determine its species. Mohs saw this as a simple means of distinguishing minerals one from another. He arranged 10 minerals according to their increasing hardness, giving each a number. The hardness of any mineral could now be determined with this scale.

ROCK TUMBLING EQUIPMENT

*MOHS SCALE OF HARDNESS

 1. TALC
 2. GYPSUM
 3. CALCITE
 4. FLUORITE
 5. APATITE
 6. FELDSPAR
7. QUARTZ
8. TOPAZ
 9. CORUNDUM
 10. DIAMOND

For example, GRAPHITE, USED IN "LEAD" PENCILS, HAS A HARDNESS OF 1 TO 2; GOLD, A HARDNESS OF 2.5 TO 3; AND OPAL, 5 TO 6.

HERB KLISCHIES '75

It Happened THIS MONTH
...EVENTS OUT OF THE PAST

WILLIAM HENRY FOX TALBOT — PIONEER IN THE INVENTION OF PHOTOGRAPHY, BORN FEBRUARY 11, 1800

Picking up a camera and snapping pictures is so common today that hardly anyone ever gives a thought to the problems that had to be solved by the pioneer photographers.

Several people had been working on the photographic process simultaneously, but unaware of one another. It was when the French inventor *Louis Daguerre* announced his system in 1839 that the Englishman **WILLIAM FOX TALBOT** spoke up, claiming priority.

A long legal battle took place between Talbot, Daguerre, and others. In the end Talbot is credited with discovering, among other things, the **NEGATIVE - POSITIVE PRINCIPLE**, which is in use to this day.

NEGATIVE / POSITIVE

A CAMERA BUILT BY TALBOT FOR HIS EARLY EXPERIMENTS

HERB KLISCHIES '75

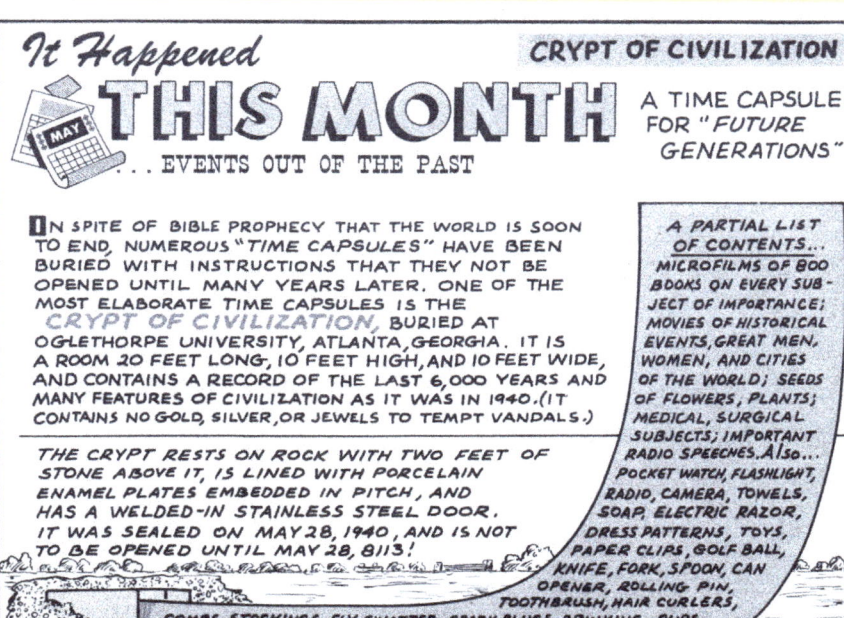

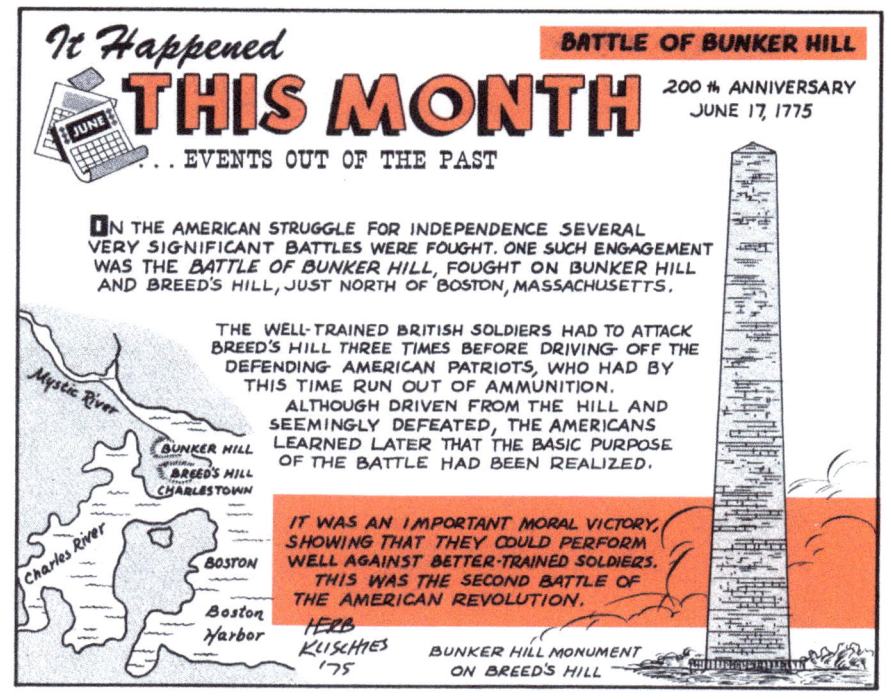

It Happened THIS MONTH
...EVENTS OUT OF THE PAST

JULY

THE MEDAL OF HONOR
"FOR CONSPICUOUS GALLANTRY... AT THE RISK OF HIS LIFE ABOVE AND BEYOND THE CALL OF DUTY"

THE MEDAL OF HONOR IS THE UNITED STATES' HIGHEST AWARD IN THE MILITARY. IT IS GIVEN FOR HEROISM IN WAR AND, OCCASIONALLY, IN PEACE. (CHARLES LINDBERGH WAS AWARDED THE MEDAL FOR HIS SOLO AIRPLANE FLIGHT ACROSS THE ATLANTIC IN 1927.) THE RESOLUTION TO MAKE SUCH AN AWARD BECAME LAW ON JULY 12, 1862. SINCE THEN MORE THAN 2,600 PERSONS HAVE RECEIVED IT, THE WINNERS COMING FROM ALL BRANCHES OF THE SERVICE.

ARMY MEDAL OF HONOR

NAVY MEDAL OF HONOR

IT WAS DURING WORLD WAR II, ON THE ISLAND OF OKINAWA, THAT A BRAVE YOUNG SOLDIER DISTINGUISHED HIMSELF AT GREAT RISK TO HIS OWN LIFE. CORPORAL DESMOND DOSS, A SEVENTH-DAY ADVENTIST MEDICAL AID MAN, SAVED MORE THAN 75 WOUNDED FELLOW SOLDIERS BY REMOVING THEM FROM THE AREA OF BATTLE TO SAFETY. PRESIDENT HARRY TRUMAN PERSONALLY MADE THE MEDAL OF HONOR AWARD DURING CEREMONIES ON THE LAWN OF THE WHITE HOUSE, WASHINGTON, D.C., OCTOBER 12, 1945.

HERB KLISCHIES '75

It Happened THIS MONTH
...EVENTS OUT OF THE PAST

AUG

GEORGES LÉOPOLD CUVIER
FRENCH NATURALIST – PIONEER IN THE STUDY OF FOSSILS.
BORN AUGUST 23, 1769

WHAT DO YOU THINK OF WHEN SOMEONE MENTIONS THE WORD "FOSSIL"? DOES IT SOUND LIKE A DRY, DULL SUBJECT? ACTUALLY, STUDYING FOSSILS CAN BE VERY EXCITING. YOU'LL DISCOVER PLANTS AND ANIMALS WHICH HAVE DISAPPEARED FROM THE EARTH MANY YEARS AGO – SUCH AS THE SABERTOOTH TIGER, THE WOOLY MAMMOTH, AND, OF COURSE, THE DINOSAUR. MANY MUSEUMS HAVE FOSSILS ON DISPLAY. IT MAY BE A FISH, A FERN, PETRIFIED WOOD, OR AN INSECT PRESERVED IN AMBER.

IN STUDYING FOSSILS, GEORGES CUVIER FIRMLY BELIEVED IN THE REGULARITY AND ORDERLINESS OF NATURE. HE WAS GENERALLY IN AGREEMENT WITH THE BIBLE ACCOUNT OF CREATION.

IF YOU HAPPEN TO BE TRAVELING THROUGH "FOSSIL COUNTRY" THIS SUMMER, KEEP YOUR EYES OPEN AND YOU MAY DISCOVER A FOSSIL ALL YOUR OWN!

FISH

TRILOBITE

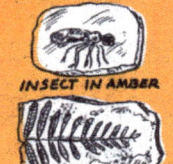

INSECT IN AMBER

FERN

REMOVING THE LEG BONES OF A DINOSAUR FROM A WYOMING FOSSIL DEPOSIT

HERB KLISCHIES '75

It Happened THIS MONTH
...EVENTS OUT OF THE PAST

AMERICAN INDIAN DAY — GENERALLY HELD ON THE FOURTH FRIDAY OF SEPTEMBER

American Indian Day

Have you ever eaten **PECANS** or **SQUASH**; seen a **CHIPMUNK**, **RACCOON**, or **MOOSE**; worn **MOCCASINS**; cracked **HICKORY** nuts; ridden on a **TOBOGGAN**, or in a **PONTIAC** automobile? These are just a few of the many words that the American Indian has given to our language. Not only in words but in deeds also did the Indians help the early settlers in America. They showed them how to plant native crops, hunt, and build shelters.

In recognition of the Indians' contributions to America, many states observe **AMERICAN INDIAN DAY**. Check with your local library or newspaper since the dates vary in some states.

— HERB KLISCHIES '75

STATE NAMES DERIVED FROM INDIAN WORDS:

ALABAMA - CREEK - TRIBAL NAME	MISSOURI - ALGONQUIAN - "PEOPLE OF THE LARGE CANOES"	OTHER STATES INCLUDE: IDAHO, ILLINOIS, IOWA, KANSAS, MASSACHUSETTS, MICHIGAN, MINNESOTA, MISSISSIPPI, NORTH AND SOUTH DAKOTA, OKLAHOMA, OREGON, UTAH, & WISCONSIN.
ALASKA - ALEUTIAN - "MAINLAND"	NEBRASKA - SIOUX - "FLAT WATER"	
ARIZONA - PAPAGO - "PLACE OF SMALL SPRING"	OHIO - IROQUOIS - "SOMETHING GREAT"	
ARKANSAS - SIOUX - "DOWNSTREAM PEOPLE"	TENNESSEE - CHEROKEE VILLAGE NAME	
CONNECTICUT - ALGONQUIAN - "PLACE OF THE LONG RIVER"	TEXAS - CADDOAN - "FRIENDS"	
KENTUCKY - IROQUOIS - "MEADOW LAND"	WYOMING - ALGONQUIAN - "UPON THE GREAT PLAIN"	

It Happened THIS MONTH
...EVENTS OUT OF THE PAST

BATTLE OF HASTINGS — ONE OF THE WORLD'S DECISIVE BATTLES — OCTOBER 14, 1066

Of all the world's battles, very few have been designated as *DECISIVE* — those which changed the course of human history. One such battle was the *BATTLE OF HASTINGS*. When Harold II was chosen King of England, William of Normandy claimed that the English throne had been promised to him. A dispute arose and both men raised armies and fought each other with crossbowmen, archers, knights, and untrained peasants at the Hill of Senlac, near Hastings, England.

Harold was killed and William became ruler of England. Had Harold been victorious, what would have been the course of history — better or worse? We don't know, but it would certainly have been different. This is why Hastings is considered a decisive battle.

— HERB KLISCHIES '75

1976

Nineteen Seventy-Six

It Happened THIS MONTH
...EVENTS OUT OF THE PAST

OLD LONDON BRIDGE

"LONDON BRIDGE IS FALLING DOWN..."

It comes as a surprise to some people to discover that there really was a London Bridge that fell down section by section— not once, but many times.

Soon after Old London Bridge was completed in the year 1209, people began building houses and shops on the bridge. Living and shopping on the bridge was a unique experience at first. As time went on, the bridge became more crowded. It began to wear out and needed repairs. Fires broke out, which meant rebuilding of sections. Finally it was decided that the whole bridge needed to come down. An old print, dated January, 1832, shows the bridge being demolished (falling down). A new bridge was taking its place.

It Happened THIS MONTH
...EVENTS OUT OF THE PAST

HEINRICH RUDOLPH HERTZ
PIONEER IN THE DEVELOPMENT OF RADIO-TELEVISION-RADAR

Look at the dial plate on your radio. Do you see these letters? MHz stands for MEGAHERTZ on the FM dial, and KHz stands for KILOHERTZ, on the AM dial. These designations are in honor of HEINRICH RUDOLPH HERTZ, whose discoveries in the field of electromagnetism led others to the development of RADIO, TELEVISION, AND RADAR.

Hertz, who was born February 22, 1857, was a German physicist and a versitile genius. Besides physics, he taught physiology, anatomy, and mathematics. He also invented the ophthalmoscope, an instrument used for eye examinations.

Hertz designed and built the kind of antenna used for television reception long before there was any television!

It Happened THIS MONTH
...EVENTS OUT OF THE PAST

JOSEPH PRIESTLEY — DISCOVERER OF OXYGEN AND OTHER GASES. BORN MARCH 13, 1733

WHEN A PERSON CARRIES ON A SCIENTIFIC EXPERIMENT, HE USUALLY KNOWS WHAT HE'S LOOKING FOR AND IS JUST TRYING TO FIND THE WAY TO ACHIEVE THAT RESULT. THERE ARE OTHER TIMES WHEN GREAT DISCOVERIES HAVE COME ABOUT BY ACCIDENT. SUCH WAS THE CASE WITH THE DISCOVERY OF **OXYGEN**.

JOSEPH PRIESTLEY, ENGLISH CLERGYMAN AND CHEMIST, WAS EXPERIMENTING WITH DIFFERENT KINDS OF AIR, WHICH HE COLLECTED IN JARS. NEARBY WAS A CANDLE. FOR NO OTHER REASON THAN JUST CURIOSITY, PRIESTLEY PUT THE CANDLE INTO THE JAR OF AIR HE HAD COLLECTED. *THE FLAME BURNED BRIGHTER!* A RED-HOT STICK FROM THE FIREPLACE BURST INTO FLAMES WHEN PUT INTO ANOTHER JAR.

IT REMAINED FOR A LATER SCIENTIST TO NAME THE GAS WHICH PRIESTLEY HAD DISCOVERED **"OXYGEN"**. OTHER DISCOVERIES BY PRIESTLEY INCLUDE **NITROUS OXIDE**, OR "LAUGHING GAS," USED BY DENTISTS, AND **CARBON DIOXIDE**, THE "FIZZ" IN SODA POP, GINGER ALE, AND ICE CREAM SODAS.

USES OF OXYGEN INCLUDE OXYGEN TENTS IN HOSPITALS, AIR TANKS FOR DIVERS, HIGH-FLYING AIRPLANES, BLOWTORCHES, ETC.

HERB KLISCHIES '76

It Happened THIS MONTH
...EVENTS OUT OF THE PAST

FIRST UNITED STATES MINT

LINCOLN CENT MINT MARKS ALWAYS ON FRONT

SINCE 1968, ALL MINT MARKS APPEAR ON THE OBVERSE (FRONT)

TAKE SOME AMERICAN COINS AND CAREFULLY LOOK AT BOTH SIDES UNTIL YOU FIND A SMALL SINGLE LETTER, EITHER A "D" OR AN "S". THESE ARE CALLED **MINT MARKS**. THE LETTER "D" MEANS THE COIN WAS MADE, OR "STRUCK," AT THE DENVER, COLORADO, MINT. THE "S" STANDS FOR SAN FRANCISCO. IF THE COIN DOESN'T HAVE A MINT MARK, IT WAS STRUCK AT THE MAIN MINT IN PHILADELPHIA, PENNSYLVANIA.

AFTER AMERICA GAINED HER INDEPENDENCE IN 1776, ONE MAJOR PROBLEM WAS ITS MONEY SYSTEM. INDIVIDUAL STATES WERE ISSUING THEIR OWN COINS, SOME COINS WERE STRUCK PRIVATELY, AND THE NEW GOVERNMENT BEGAN EXPERIMENTING WITH ITS OWN COINS.

TO PUT COINAGE ON A SOUNDER BASIS, A RESOLUTION PROVIDING FOR THE ESTABLISHMENT OF A NATIONAL MINT WAS SIGNED INTO LAW APRIL 2, 1792. THE FEDERAL GOVERNMENT ALONE WOULD NOW PRODUCE ALL COINS.

FIRST LARGE CENTS (1793) STRUCK AT FIRST UNITED STATES MINT - PHILADELPHIA

PRODUCTION OF THE DOLLAR WAS HALTED IN 1935 AND RESUMED IN 1971 WITH THE EISENHOWER DOLLAR

HERB KLISCHIES '76

1976 • Page 157

It Happened THIS MONTH
...EVENTS OUT OF THE PAST

CONFEDERATE MEMORIAL

CARVING AT STONE MOUNTAIN, GEORGIA
DEPICTING (LEFT TO RIGHT) JEFFERSON DAVIS, ROBERT E. LEE "STONEWALL" JACKSON

THE WORLD'S LARGEST SINGLE PIECE OF SCULPTURAL ART IS THE **CONFEDERATE MEMORIAL** CARVING ON THE SIDE OF **STONE MOUNTAIN**, LOCATED 20 MILES EAST OF ATLANTA, GEORGIA.
  CARVING THE GRANITE WAS BEGUN IN THE EARLY 1920's, BUT ABANDONED A FEW YEARS LATER. A SECOND ATTEMPT WAS HALTED IN 1928 BECAUSE OF FINANCIAL PROBLEMS. WORK WASN'T RESUMED UNTIL 1964. USING MODERN EQUIPMENT, THE PROJECT WAS COMPLETED IN MAY, 1970.

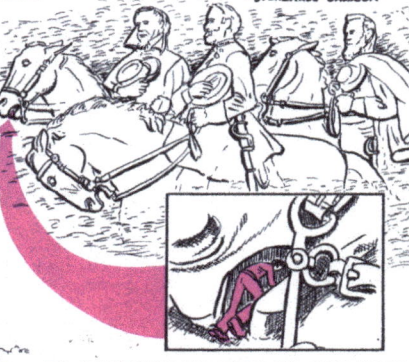

TO GIVE YOU AN IDEA OF JUST HOW LARGE THE CARVING IS, IF YOU ARE UNDER SIX FEET TALL YOU COULD STAND IN THE MOUTH OF DAVIS' HORSE!

A CABLE CAR RIDE TO THE TOP OF STONE MOUNTAIN GIVES YOU A GOOD CLOSE-UP VIEW OF THE CARVING.

HERB KLISCHIES '76

It Happened THIS MONTH
...EVENTS OUT OF THE PAST

200th ANNIVERSARY — 1776-1976

The **LIBERTY BELL** ALSO KNOWN AS "OLD STATE HOUSE BELL," "BELL OF THE REVOLUTION," AND "OLD INDEPENDENCE."

"PROCLAIM LIBERTY THROUGHOUT ALL THE LAND UNTO ALL THE INHABITANTS THEREOF" LEV. 25:10
INSCRIPTION ON THE LIBERTY BELL

ONE OF THE MOST TREASURED RELICS OF THE AMERICAN REVOLUTION IS THE **LIBERTY BELL** — SO NAMED BECAUSE IT WAS RUNG JULY 8, 1776, TO ANNOUNCE THAT THE **DECLARATION OF INDEPENDENCE** HAD BEEN ADOPTED.
  THE LIBERTY BELL BEGAN AS AN ORDINARY BELL, CAST IN ENGLAND. UPON ITS ARRIVAL IN PHILADELPHIA IN 1752 IT CRACKED WHILE BEING TESTED. TWO LOCAL IRONWORKERS RECAST THE BELL. THE NEW BELL JANGLED SO MUCH WHEN STRUCK THAT A THIRD BELL WAS CAST. THIS IS THE BELL WHICH RANG IN JULY, 1776, AND EACH JULY 4 UNTIL 1835, WHEN THE PRESENT CRACK APPEARED.

HAD NOT THE BELL CRACKED WHEN FIRST TESTED, IT WOULD HAVE THE NAME WHITECHAPEL FOUNDRY (ENGLAND) ON IT. INSTEAD, IT BEARS THE NAMES OF TWO HUMBLE AMERICAN IRONWORKERS — **JOHN PASS** AND **CHARLES STOW**.
HAPPY BIRTHDAY, AMERICA — MAY LIBERTY CONTINUE TO BE PROCLAIMED THROUGHOUT THE LAND!

HERB KLISCHIES '76

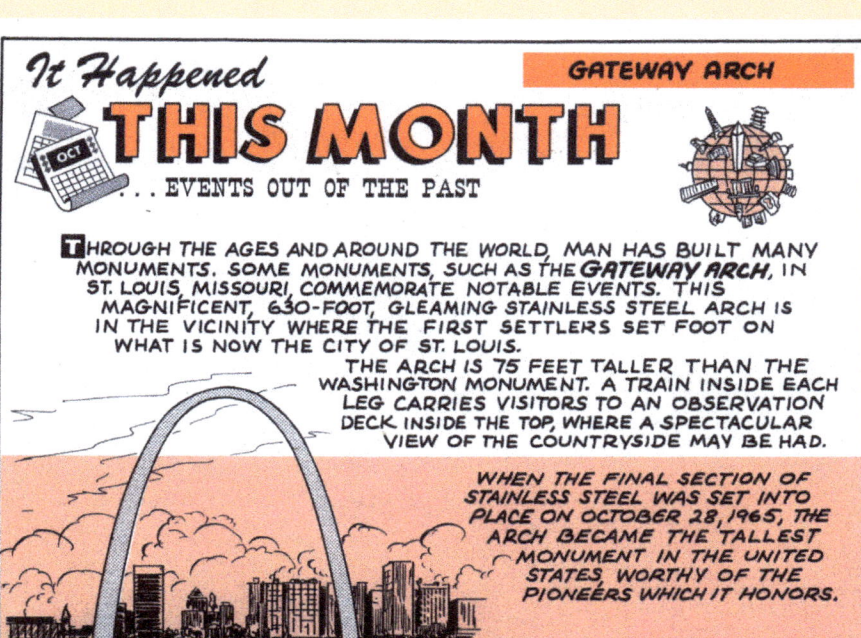

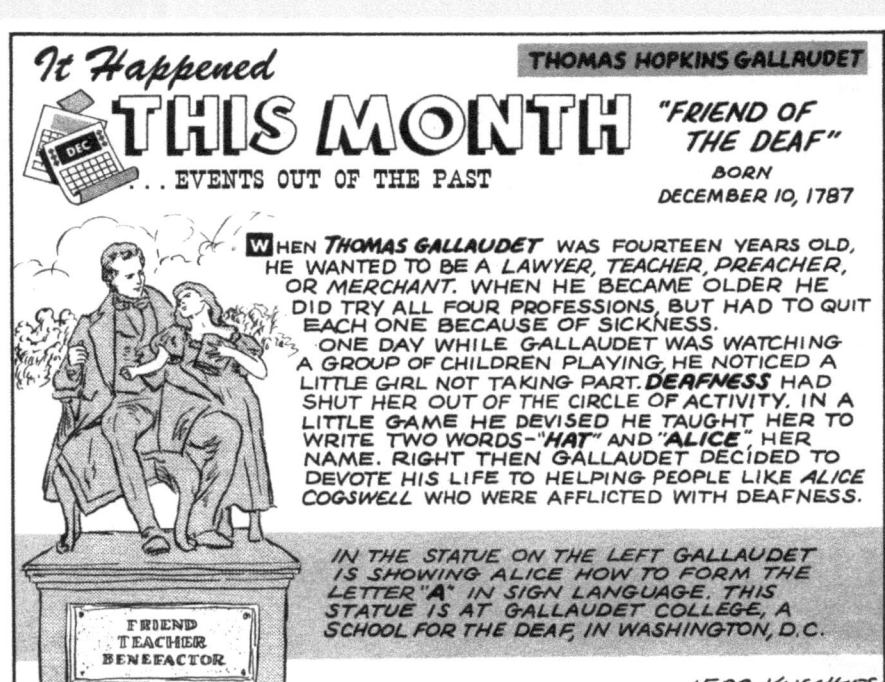

1977

Nineteen Seventy-Seven

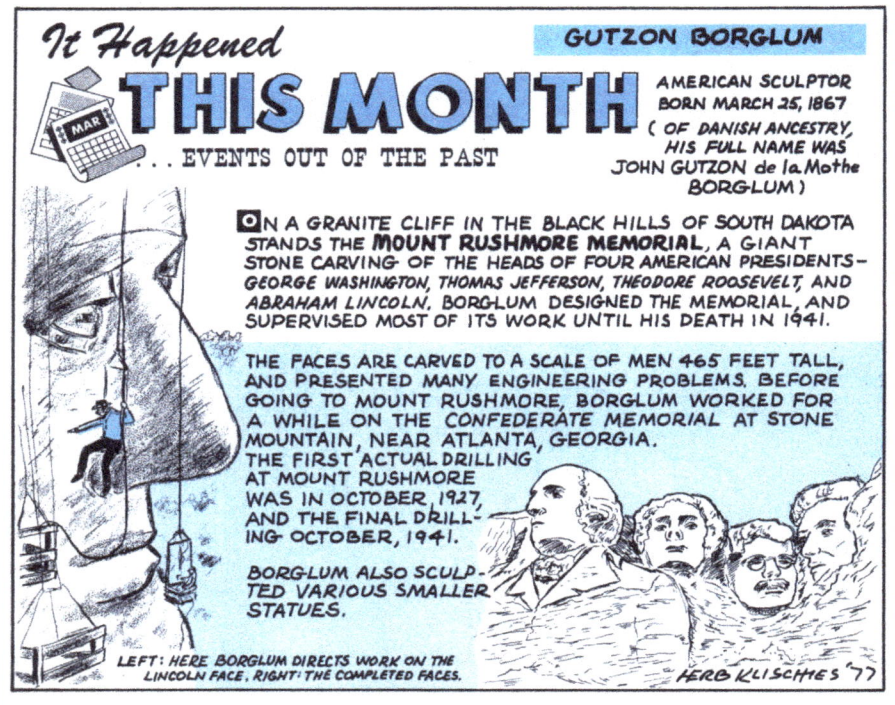

It Happened THIS MONTH
...EVENTS OUT OF THE PAST

 GIDEONS INTERNATIONAL

IF YOU HAVE EVER BEEN IN A MOTEL, HOTEL, OR HOSPITAL ROOM, OR HAVE VISITED A JAIL, AND HAVE SEEN A BIBLE LYING ON A DESK, IT WAS PROBABLY PLACED THERE BY A MEMBER OF THE **GIDEONS INTERNATIONAL**. THIS IS AN INTERDENOMINATIONAL RELIGIOUS ASSOCIATION OF CHRISTIAN BUSINESS AND PROFESSIONAL MEN WHOSE PRIMARY WORK IS THE PLACEMENT OF BIBLES IN VARIOUS ESTABLISHMENTS. GIDEONS INTERNATIONAL WAS ORGANIZED AT JANESVILLE, WISCONSIN, ON JULY 1, 1899. IN 1908, THE ORGANIZATION BEGAN PLACING BIBLES IN HOTEL ROOMS FOR THE BENEFIT OF TRAVELING MEN. TODAY THE GIDEONS ARE ACTIVE IN MORE THAN 100 COUNTRIES, HAVING DISTRIBUTED (SINCE 1908) MORE THAN **150 MILLION** COPIES OF THE KING JAMES VERSION OF THE **BIBLE**, AND SMALLER VOLUMES CONTAINING THE **NEW TESTAMENT, PSALMS,** AND **PROVERBS**.

THE ORGANIZATION'S EMBLEM, WHICH SIGNIFIES GIDEON'S VICTORY OVER THE MIDIANITES AS RECORDED IN JUDGES 7.

"IT HAPPENED THIS MONTH" IS TWENTY YEARS OLD. AT LEFT IS THE FIRST DRAWING AS IT APPEARED IN JULY, 1957. MY SINCERE THANKS GO TO ELDER LAWRENCE MAXWELL, GUIDE'S FIRST EDITOR, WHO AGREED TO TAKE ON MY FEATURE, AND TO ELDER LOWELL LITTEN, GUIDE'S PRESENT EDITOR, FOR LETTING IT CONTINUE.

HERB KLISCHIES '77

It Happened THIS MONTH
...EVENTS OUT OF THE PAST

 "GREENBACKS"

YOU'VE PROBABLY HEARD THE EXPRESSION "**GREENBACK**" IN REFERRING TO UNITED STATES **PAPER MONEY**. THIS NAME ORIGINATED WITH THE **DEMAND NOTES** OF 1861, THE FIRST PAPER MONEY ISSUED BY THE UNITED STATES GOVERNMENT. BECAUSE OF THE **COLOR** OF THE REVERSE, THEY IMMEDIATELY BECAME KNOWN AS **GREENBACKS**.

THE TECHNICAL NAME IS **DEMAND NOTES** AND COMES FROM THE FOLLOWING ON THE FRONT OF THE NOTES: "THE UNITED STATES PROMISE TO PAY TO THE BEARER (5, 10, OR 20) DOLLARS ON DEMAND."

THESE NOTES CARRIED THE PHRASE "ACT OF JULY 17, 1861," AND ALSO THE ADDITIONAL DATE OF **AUGUST 10TH, 1861**, WHICH IS PROBABLY THE ACTUAL DATE OF ISSUE TO THE PUBLIC.

HERB KLISCHIES '77

1977 • Page 167

It Happened THIS MONTH
...EVENTS OUT OF THE PAST

HIRAM PERCY MAXIM
Founder of the AMERICAN RADIO RELAY LEAGUE (ARRL)
BORN SEPTEMBER 2, 1869

ARE YOU A "HAM"?

YOU ARE IF YOU OPERATE AN **AMATEUR RADIO STATION**. HAM RADIO IS NOT ONLY A FASCINATING HOBBY BUT CAN ALSO BE VERY HELPFUL IN CASE OF **DISASTER**. WHEN FLOODS, TORNADOS, EARTHQUAKES, OR SNOW STORMS DISABLE REGULAR RADIO AND TELEVISION BROADCASTING, AMATEURS FREQUENTLY ARE THE ONLY MEANS OF OUTSIDE COMMUNICATION AND PLAY AN IMPORTANT PART IN DIRECTING **EMERGENCY RELIEF** TO THE STRICKEN AREA.

THE **ARRL** IS DEDICATED TO THE PROGRESS OF AMATEUR RADIO. AS PRESIDENT OF THE ORGANIZATION FROM 1914 TO 1936, MAXIM DID MUCH TO STRENGTHEN THE POSITION OF AMATEUR RADIO IN THE UNITED STATES. TODAY, THIS WORLD-WIDE HOBBY IS ENJOYED BY GRADE SCHOOL STUDENT AND SENIOR CITIZEN ALIKE.

73's TO YOU! (ASK A HAM WHAT THIS MEANS)

HERB KLISCHIES '77

It Happened THIS MONTH
...EVENTS OUT OF THE PAST

WORLD'S OLDEST "CAR"
DESIGNED AND BUILT BY NICHOLAS JOSEPH CUGNOT
FRENCH ENGINEER

FOR THOUSANDS OF YEARS PEOPLE HAVE USED HORSES AND OTHER ANIMALS TO PULL WAGONS AND CARRIAGES. THE IDEA OF HAVING A WAGON MOVE **WITHOUT** USING HORSES CAUSED MANY TO TRY AND BUILD SUCH A WAGON.

THE ODD-LOOKING MACHINE AT RIGHT IS RECOGNIZED AS THE WORLD'S **FIRST SELF-PROPELLED VEHICLE**." IT WAS INTENDED TO DRAG CANNON ONTO THE BATTLEFIELD. CUGNOT SUCCESSFULLY DEMONSTRATED A SMALLER PROTOTYPE OF THIS VEHICLE IN PARIS, FRANCE, IN OCTOBER, 1769. HE WAS THEN ORDERED TO CONSTRUCT A FULL-SIZED WAGON, WHICH HE DID IN 1770 — THE RATHER CLUMSY, 3-WHEELED, STEAM-DRIVEN TRUCK SHOWN HERE, AND NOW ON DISPLAY IN A PARIS MUSEUM.

* CONFLICTING REPORTS MAKE IT UNCLEAR AS TO WHETHER OR NOT THIS PARTICULAR MACHINE EVER MOVED UNDER ITS OWN POWER. (CUGNOT'S PROTOTYPE DID.) ONE REPORT STATED THAT IT WENT ABOUT **2½ MILES AN HOUR!** But, IT WAS A BEGINNING, HOWEVER CRUDE, AND FROM SUCH A SMALL BEGINNING EVOLVED THE WORLD-WIDE INDUSTRY OF **SELF-PROPELLED VEHICLES** — AUTOMOBILES, TRUCKS, BUSSES, MOTORCYCLES, ETC.

HERB KLISCHIES '77

It Happened THIS MONTH
...EVENTS OUT OF THE PAST

MARIE CURIE — POLISH SCIENTIST. CO-WORKER IN THE DISCOVERY OF RADIUM

ONE OF THE GREATEST OF THE WORLD'S SCIENTISTS AND CERTAINLY THE GREATEST WOMAN SCIENTIST IN THE WORLD WAS **MARIE CURIE**, WHO, ALONG WITH HER HUSBAND **PIERRE**, DISCOVERED **RADIUM**, THE ELEMENT USED IN THE TREATMENT OF MANY DISEASES.

MARIE SKLODOWSKA CURIE WAS BORN IN WARSAW, POLAND, NOVEMBER 7, 1867. HER FATHER TAUGHT PHYSICS AND MATHEMATICS, SO MARIE LEARNED AT AN EARLY AGE THAT WHICH WAS TO HELP HER IN HER LIFE'S WORK.

"THE DISCOVERY OF RADIUM AND OF RADIOACTIVE SUBSTANCES MARKED THE OPENING OF **THE ATOMIC AGE**"

FOR THEIR DISCOVERY OF RADIUM, THE CURIES RECEIVED THE **NOBEL PRIZE FOR PHYSICS** IN 1903. IN 1911, MARIE CURIE RECEIVED THE **NOBEL PRIZE IN CHEMISTRY** FOR ISOLATING RADIUM. IT WAS THE FIRST TIME THAT THE PRIZE WAS AWARDED TWICE TO THE SAME PERSON. SHE ALSO RECEIVED MANY OTHER SCIENTIFIC PRIZES, AWARDS, MEDALS, AND HONORARY TITLES.

THE CHEMISTRY AND PHYSICS MEDALS HAVE THE SAME REVERSE SIDES

HERB KLISCHIES '77

It Happened THIS MONTH
...EVENTS OUT OF THE PAST

NOBEL PRIZES

EACH YEAR ON DECEMBER 10, AND USUALLY IN STOCKHOLM, SWEDEN, SEVERAL VERY IMPORTANT AWARDS ARE MADE. THESE ARE THE **NOBEL PRIZES**,* WHICH ARE GIVEN TO PERSONS, REGARDLESS OF NATIONALITY, WHO HAVE WORKED FOR THE BENEFIT OF MANKIND AND HAVE MADE OUTSTANDING CONTRIBUTIONS IN FIVE AREAS —

OBVERSE OF NOBEL PEACE PRIZE MEDALLION

| CHEMISTRY | LITERATURE | PEACE | PHYSICS | PHYSIOLOGY-MEDICINE |

*EACH PRIZE INCLUDES A GOLD MEDAL, A DIPLOMA, AND MONEY (IN 1974 THE VALUE WAS $124,000).

ALFRED BERNHARD NOBEL WAS A SWEDISH CHEMIST WHO INVENTED DYNAMITE AND OTHER EXPLOSIVES FOR PEACEFUL PURPOSES. BEFORE LONG PEOPLE USED HIS EXPLOSIVES FOR WAR RATHER THAN PEACE.

WHEN NOBEL DIED ON DECEMBER 10, 1896, HIS WILL OUTLINED A PLAN FOR THE DISTRIBUTION OF HIS WEALTH. THE INTEREST ON HIS FORTUNE OF ABOUT $9,000,000 WOULD BE DIVIDED INTO FIVE EQUAL PARTS AMONG THE FIVE PERSONS WHO HAD MADE VALUABLE CONTRIBUTIONS TO THE GOOD OF HUMANITY. THE AWARDS WERE FIRST MADE ON DECEMBER 10, 1901, THE FIFTH ANNIVERSARY OF NOBEL'S DEATH.

HERB KLISCHIES '77

1978

Nineteen Seventy-Eight

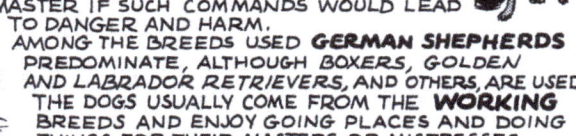

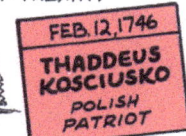

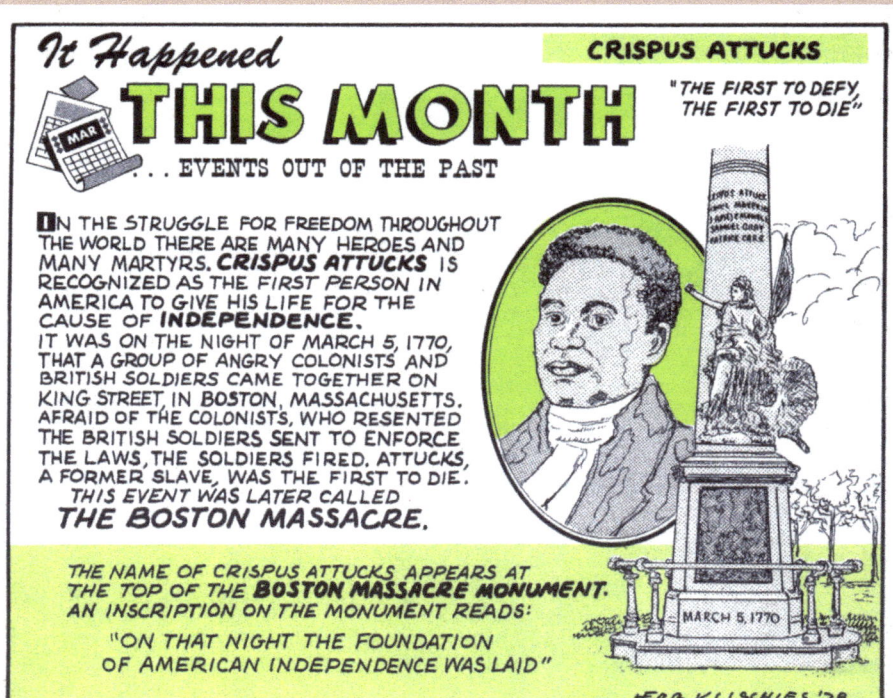

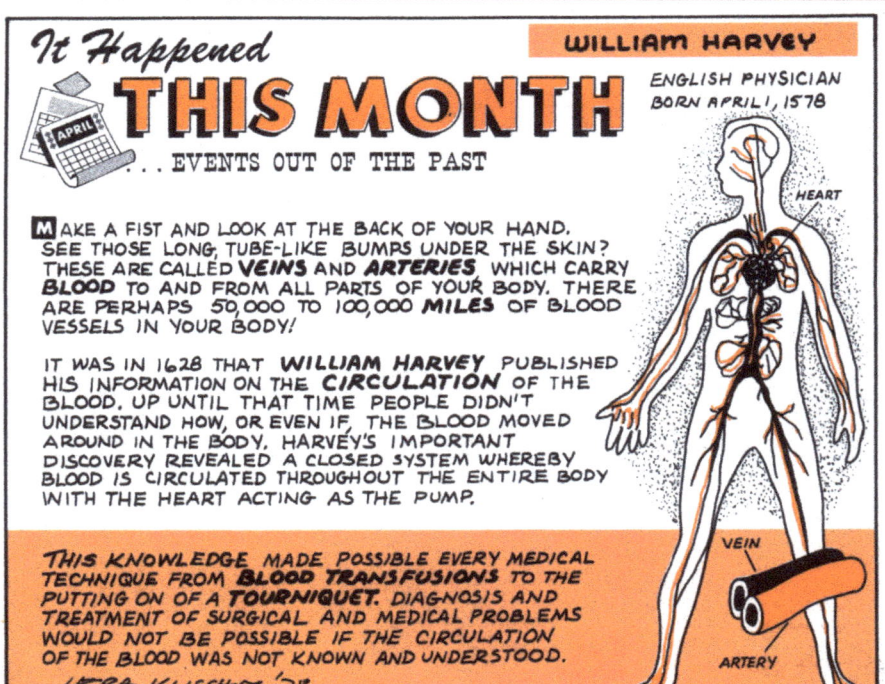

It Happened  THIS MONTH
...EVENTS OUT OF THE PAST

EDWARD JENNER — ENGLISH PHYSICIAN BORN MAY 17, 1749. CONQUEROR OF SMALLPOX DISEASE.

SMALLPOX IS A DISEASE THAT ONCE CAUSED MUCH SICKNESS AND DEATH AROUND THE WORLD. TODAY IT HAS BEEN VIRTUALLY ELIMINATED, THANKS TO THE UNTIRING EFFORTS OF **EDWARD JENNER**. DR. JENNER NOTICED THAT ANYONE WHO HAD HAD **COWPOX**, A MILDER DISEASE, DID NOT CATCH **SMALLPOX**. HE REASONED THAT SUCH A PERSON WAS **IMMUNE**. JENNER WANTED TO IMMUNIZE PEOPLE BY USING COWPOX VACCINE, BUT AT FIRST HE WAS JEERED AND RIDICULED. SINCE THE VACCINE CAME FROM A COW, PEOPLE SAID THEY WOULD **"MOO"** INSTEAD OF TALK, AND EVEN **GROW HORNS!** FOR **25 YEARS** JENNER STOOD FIRM. GRADUALLY HIS VACCINATION METHOD BECAME MORE ACCEPTABLE AS THE NUMBER OF SMALLPOX CASES DECLINED.

JAMES PHIPPS, AN 8-YEAR-OLD BOY, RECEIVED THE FIRST VACCINE FROM JENNER IN MAY, 1796. HE DID NOT CATCH THE DISEASE. **JENNER'S THEORY PROVED CORRECT!**

HERB KLISCHIES '78

It Happened  THIS MONTH
...EVENTS OUT OF THE PAST

JOHN HOWARD PAYNE — AUTHOR OF "HOME, SWEET HOME"

"'MID PLEASURES AND PALACES THOUGH WE MAY ROAM, BE IT EVER SO HUMBLE, THERE'S NO PLACE LIKE HOME..."

SO BEGINS ONE OF AMERICA'S MOST BELOVED SONGS — "**HOME, SWEET HOME**". ITS AUTHOR, **JOHN HOWARD PAYNE**, WAS AN ACTOR WHO WANDERED AROUND THE WORLD. WHILE IN LONDON, ENGLAND, PAYNE NEEDED MONEY. HE SOLD SOME OF HIS WRITINGS TO A MUSIC PUBLISHER, INCLUDING THE POEM "**HOME, SWEET HOME**". SOON AFTER BEING SET TO MUSIC THE SONG BECAME VERY POPULAR BECAUSE IT STRUCK A RESPONSIVE CHORD IN THE HEARTS OF ALL WHO HEARD IT. NO MATTER HOW HUMBLE IT MAY BE — **THERE'S NO PLACE LIKE HOME!**

PAYNE WAS BORN JUNE 9, 1791, IN EAST HAMPTON, LONG ISLAND, NEW YORK. HIS BOYHOOD HOME STILL STANDS TODAY, AND YOU CAN VISIT IT. IT IS A **SALTBOX-STYLE** FARMHOUSE, BUILT IN 1660.

HERB KLISCHIES '78

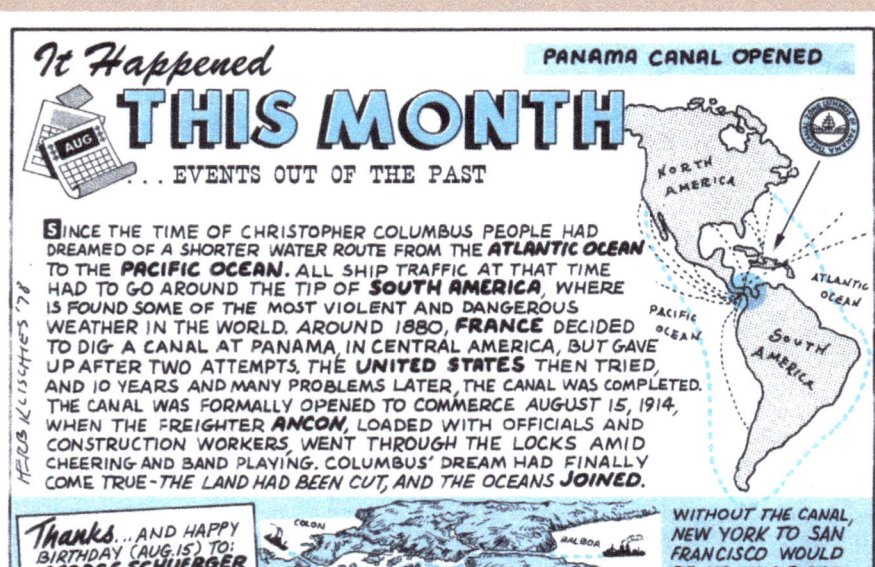

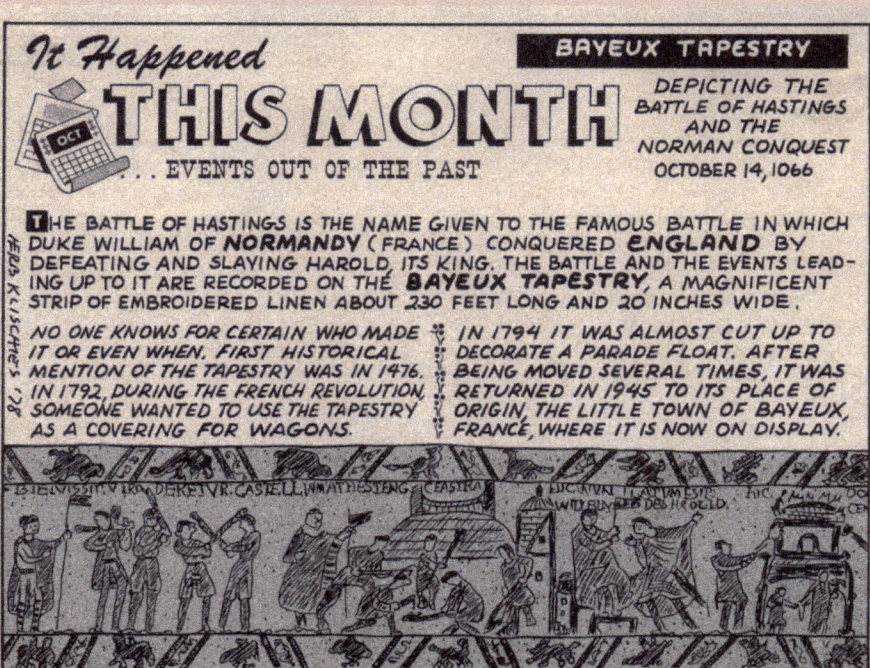

It Happened THIS MONTH
...EVENTS OUT OF THE PAST

AUGUSTE RODIN
FRENCH SCULPTOR
BORN NOVEMBER 4, 1840
PARIS, FRANCE

Perhaps you have never heard of the French sculptor **AUGUSTE RODIN**, but it is very likely that you have seen a reproduction of one of his most well-known figures —**THE THINKER**— shown here. It has been reproduced for many different purposes, both serious and frivolous.

But THE THINKER is only one of thousands of figures and groups which Rodin produced as a sculptor. He was also a prolific **ARTIST**, painting in both watercolor and oils.

RODIN WAS CONSIDERED THE GREATEST FRENCH SCULPTOR OF HIS TIME (FROM 1877 TO 1917).

HERB KLISCHES '78

It Happened THIS MONTH
...EVENTS OUT OF THE PAST

SIR ISAAC NEWTON
ENGLISH MATHEMATICIAN AND ASTRONOMER
BORN DECEMBER 25, 1642

Rockets and **SATELLITES** of today have been made possible because of the work of a great scientist who lived more than 250 years ago — **SIR ISAAC NEWTON**. Newton is best remembered for formulating the **LAW OF GRAVITY** after watching an apple fall from a tree. **GRAVITY**, as you know, must be overcome in order for rockets to break loose from the earth's pull as they travel into **SPACE**.

NEWTON IS ALSO CREDITED WITH MANY OTHER ACCOMPLISHMENTS OF ALMOST EQUAL IMPORTANCE:
- MAJOR DISCOVERIES IN THE FIELD OF **MATHEMATICS**.
- CONSTRUCTION OF A REFLECTING **TELESCOPE**.
- EXPERIMENTS WITH **PRISMS** AND **LIGHT**, SHOWING THAT **WHITE LIGHT** IS MADE UP OF THE **SEVEN COLORS** OF THE RAINBOW.

VIOLET, INDIGO, BLUE, GREEN, YELLOW, ORANGE, RED

BECAUSE OF HIS CONTRIBUTIONS, WHICH FORM THE BASIS FOR MODERN SCIENCE, NEWTON HAS BEEN CALLED A "**MASTERMIND**." BUT HE SAID HE WAS LIKE A BOY FINDING A FEW PEBBLES ON A BEACH WHILE THE GREAT OCEAN OF UNDISCOVERED KNOWLEDGE LAY ALL AROUND HIM...

HERB KLISCHES '78

1979

Nineteen Seventy-Nine

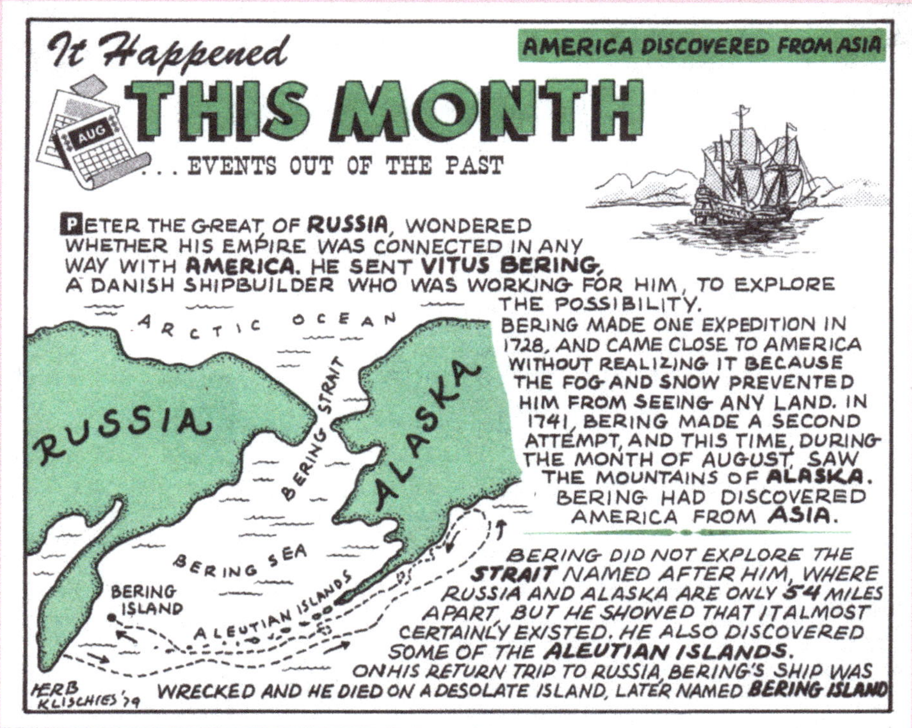

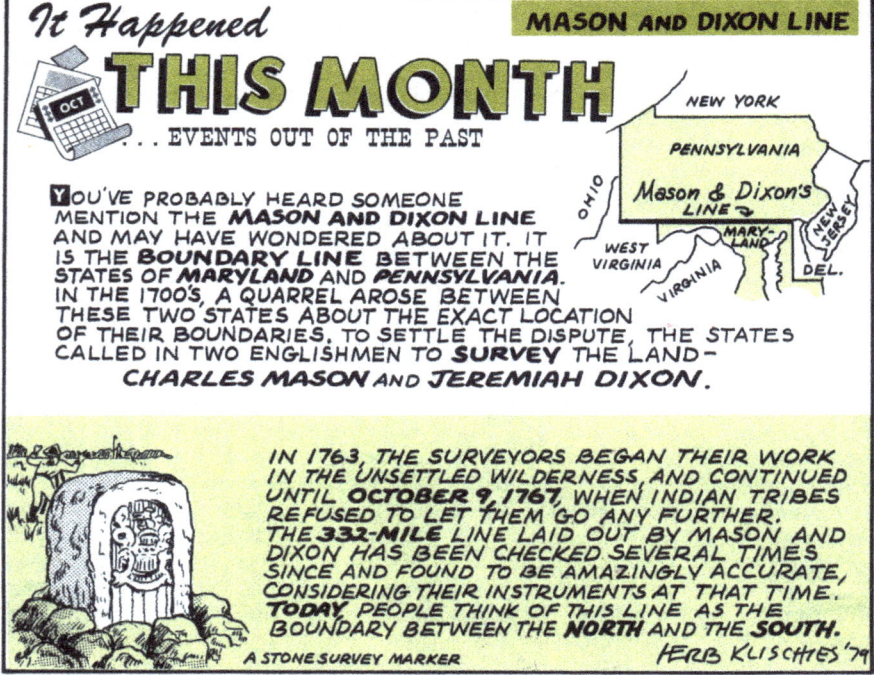

It Happened THIS MONTH
...EVENTS OUT OF THE PAST

MARIE FRANCOIS XAVIER BICHAT
FRENCH ANATOMIST AND PHYSIOLOGIST
BORN NOVEMBER 11, 1771

Proper **TOOLS** and **EQUIPMENT** enable a person to do good work, but when a person does great things **WITHOUT** such equipment his accomplishments are all the more remarkable. Such was the case with **DR. BICHAT**, who, working before **MICROSCOPES** had been perfected, became successful as an **ANATOMIST, PHYSIOLOGIST, PHYSICIAN,** and **SURGEON**. Besides this, he was teaching, dissecting, and running an extensive private practice.

Bichat was one of the founders of the science of **HISTOLOGY**, which is the study of the microscopic **STRUCTURE OF ORGANIC TISSUES**. His conclusions in his scientific studies were based on his keen unaided-eye observations of various **ORGANS** and **TISSUES**.

HERB KLISCHES '79

It Happened THIS MONTH
...EVENTS OUT OF THE PAST

SIR RICHARD ARKWRIGHT
ENGLISH MANUFACTURER
BORN DECEMBER 23, 1732

In our modern life many kinds of **MACHINES** do our work, for which we're thankful. But in the **1760'S**, people were afraid that the new **THREAD-SPINNING** machines would put many who spun thread by hand out of work. So worried were some that they **DESTROYED** any machine they could find. The inventors had to hide their inventions for fear of the angry people.

ARKWRIGHT'S FIRST SPINNING FRAME

During this period, Arkwright invented several machines that worked together to produce **COTTON THREAD**. He put uncleaned cotton into the first machine, and from the last one (the **WATER FRAME**) came clean, well-twisted thread. This was the first **COTTON MILL** and the beginning of the **FACTORY SYSTEM**.

So, instead of putting people **OUT** of work, machines provided many jobs and brought the price down on formerly expensive hand-produced items.

WATER FRAME, DRIVEN BY WATER POWER

HERB KLISCHES '79

HOW "IT HAPPENED" HAPPENS

HERB KLISCHIES
PHOTOS SUPPLIED BY AUTHOR

HI. I'M Herb Klischies and I draw the GUIDE feature "It Happened This Month." People have asked me through the years, "Where do you get your ideas?" or "How do you put a drawing like that together?" This little picture story is in answer to those and other questions you may have.

Many sources for ideas are available. One is the newspaper column listing several events that took place on the same month and day in past years. Other sources are advertisements commemorating an anniversary by a particular company. As an example, a gas company stated in one of its ads, "On June 18, 1861, our company provided gas for the first military balloon." (This item appeared in GUIDE, June, 1966.) Some encyclopedias have sections describing happenings that occurred during each month of the year. And there are other books that list historic events that have taken place on each day of the year.

After looking over what I think you would enjoy reading, I clip the ads, or make note of book pages, and file them for future reference. I have a file folder for each month, and whenever I come across something of interest I save it (Picture 1).

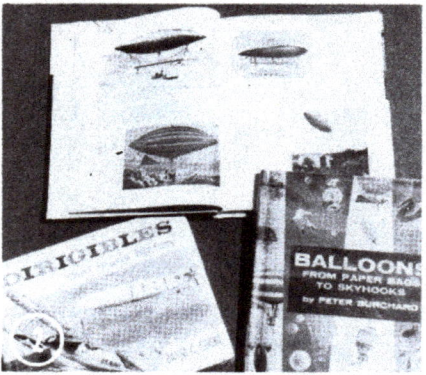

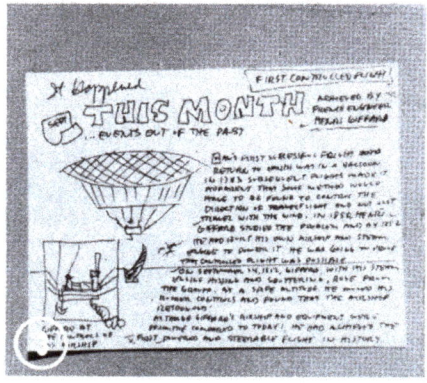

As an actual example, let me show you how this month's feature came into being. In looking through my folder for September I came across the name of Henri Giffard, who achieved

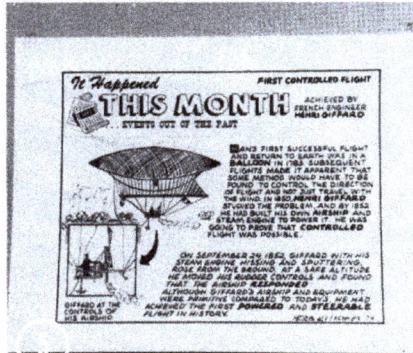

the material into two or three paragraphs. I make what is called a layout, which contains the wording and roughly drawn illustration as it's going to appear (Picture 3). I send this layout to the GUIDE editor, where it is checked for accuracy—dates, grammar, sentence structure. Within a week or so the layout is returned, with necessary correction or change. Now I'm able to do the final artwork, using the layout for a guide (Picture 4).

On a piece of drawing board about twice the size of what will appear in GUIDE I start my artwork. The artwork is done larger because it's easier to work with, and becomes sharper when reduced. With a light-blue pen, the ink of which doesn't photograph, I indicate where the illustrations and the lettering are to go. Then, using black India ink, I letter the words carefully. With either pen or brush, I complete the illustrations. Several hours later I'm finished (Picture 5).

I look over the completed artwork for mistakes, which sometimes seem to happen, then add the color overlay. This is a sheet of thin clear plastic that shows the photo-offset photographer what areas are to be in color.

The finished drawing and original layout are then sent to the editor. When Elder Litten receives the drawing he looks it over once more, then if everything is OK, sends it on its way through the various departments of the Review and Herald Publishing Association, and it finally emerges in your GUIDE as shown on page 11.

That's about it. I hope this has helped you understand a little better some of the work that goes into something as simple-looking as "It Happened This Month."

And by the way, I want to thank all you juniors, earliteens, and others who have been reading this feature for the past 22 years.

the first controllable flight in history. I had been doing some research on Alberto Santos-Dumont for July and, in going through one of the books on the history of balloons, found that Giffard was the first to control balloon flight. I thought that was interesting, so a note went into my September file for future reference.

Having decided on my subject, I got several books from the library describing the history of balloons and airships (Picture 2). Sometimes I go through as many as five or six books to get as much information as possible. Then, after all that reading I condense

1980

Nineteen Eighty

It Happened THIS MONTH
...EVENTS OUT OF THE PAST

MARCO POLO
VENETIAN TRADER AND TRAVELER
DIED JANUARY 9, 1324

THE FIRST REAL INFORMATION THAT **EUROPEANS** HAD ABOUT THE **ORIENT** CAME FROM A BOOK WRITTEN BY THE VENETIAN TRAVELER, **MARCO POLO.** IN 1271, WHEN POLO WAS 17 YEARS OLD, HE, ALONG WITH HIS FATHER AND UNCLE, MADE A JOURNEY ACROSS ASIA TO **CHINA**, AND THE VAST KINGDOM OF **KUBLAI KHAN**, ITS RULER. HERE HE SAW AND RECORDED MANY STRANGE AND WONDERFUL THINGS SUCH AS BLACK STONES THAT BURNED (COAL), AND HUGE SERPENTS WITH GLARING EYES AND SHARP TEETH (CROCODILES). HE ALSO TOLD OF BEAUTIFUL CITIES AND GREAT WEALTH.

MANY PEOPLE REFUSED TO BELIEVE THESE STORIES. LATER, WHEN POLO BECAME ILL, HIS FRIENDS URGED HIM TO CONFESS THESE "LIES" BEFORE HE DIED. TO THESE HE RESPONDED —
*"I HAVE NOT TOLD YOU EVEN **HALF** OF WHAT I SAW!"*

LATER EXPLORATIONS BY OTHERS CONFIRMED THAT WHAT MARCO POLO HAD WRITTEN ABOUT WAS A TRUE ACCOUNT OF HIS GREAT ADVENTURES

POLO BEFORE THE MIGHTY MONGOL RULER, **KUBLAI KHAN**

MARCO POLO LEARNS ABOUT THE GREAT WALL OF CHINA

HERB KLISCHIES '80

We invite you to view the complete
selection of titles we publish at:

www.TEACHServices.com

scan with your mobile
device to go directly
to our website

Please write or email us your praises, reactions, or
thoughts about this or any other book we publish at:

11 Quartermaster Circle
Fort Oglethorpe, GA 30742

Info@TEACHServices.com

TEACH Services, Inc., titles may be purchased in bulk for
educational, business, fund-raising, or sales promotional use.
For information, please e-mail:

BulkSales@TEACHServices.com

Finally if you are interested in seeing
your own book in print, please contact us at

publishing@TEACHServices.com

We would be happy to review your manuscript for free.

www.ingramcontent.com/pod-product-compliance
Lightning Source LLC
Chambersburg PA
CBHW050847240426
43667CB00022B/2950